D0516323

CERAMIC AND STONE TILING

A Complete Guide

CERAMIC AND STONE TILING

A Complete Guide

JOHN RIPLEY

THE CROWOOD PRESS

First published in 2005 by
The Crowood Press Ltd
Ramsbury, Marlborough
Wiltshire SN8 2HR

www.crowood.com

This impression 2008

British Library Cataloguing-in-Publication Data
A catalogue record for this book is available from the British Library.

ISBN 978 1 86126 777 1

Acknowledgements
We wish to thank the following companies and individuals for providing assistance with and/or material for this book.

A. Andrews and Sons (Marbles and Tiles) Ltd
For permission to take many of the photographs, both in their showroom and on site. In particular Ian Taylor, David Clough, Colin Pogson & Colin Wood and his staff.

Schlüter-Systems Ltd
For kindly providing photographs from their trim and accessory catalogue and price list.

R.H. (Dick) Fletcher
For checking the text for technical slip-ups and for his suggestions.

K.D. Denton
For making sure that the natural stone section was technically accurate.

Last but certainly not least, **David Fretwell** and **Olwyn Raper** for putting up with having their photographs taken whilst trying to get on with the job.

FRONTISPIECE: A small area of intense colour can give tremendous impact to a room.

Designed and typeset by Focus Publishing, Sevenoaks, Kent

Printed and bound in Malaysia by Times Offset (M) Sdn bhd

Contents

Tiling can be complicated! Second-century Roman mosaic. Villa del Casali, Sicily.

Preface

As is the case with most technical subjects, tiling is a much bigger field than is generally appreciated. It is more than just the tiles in modern kitchens and the large utilitarian ceramic tiles on the floors of shopping centres. It covers a huge range of materials and techniques. The pictorial mosaic work of the Roman and Byzantine empires and the incredibly complicated geometric designs of the Islamic world are all examples of the tiler's skill.

Today, as with most skilled trades, fixing systems are changing due to commercial pressure. Techniques and skills that were once commonplace are now rare and in some cases are in danger of being lost altogether.

For nearly fifty years I have been privileged to work with some of the best tilers in the business, many of them now dead. Although this book doesn't attempt to cover more than the rudiments of the trade, it couldn't have been written without the knowledge acquired from the many fine tradesmen it has been my privilege to work with over the years.

ABOVE: Even if it is not your taste, a traditional style always looks good.

LEFT: A more traditional look tends to date less quickly than the latest trend.

Introduction

The object of this book is to provide information that will enable a beginner to carry out tiling work to a satisfactory standard and to present the more competent do-it-yourself enthusiast with more detailed instructions than he or she might normally encounter. This book is definitely not intended to be a manual for the professional tiler. That would involve going into a depth of detail which is unnecessary for domestic work and which would probably bore anyone not directly involved in the trade.

There are many excellent books available that will provide enough information to enable you to carry out a competent tiling job for most domestic situations. Unfortunately, they rarely deal with the problems which we find ourselves facing in real life. This book contains plenty of information which will help you to avoid or overcome the difficulties that are most likely to crop up when doing actual tiling projects. Knowing how to do something is one thing. But knowing why it is done in that particular way enables you to understand the procedures involved in tiling and, hopefully, to foresee the problems that can arise.

Whilst it is not possible to give detailed instructions on how to overcome every difficulty, this book aims to give an insight into the processes involved and, in particular, what situations should be avoided. This, it is hoped, will provide sufficient information to assist you in making informed decisions on what needs to be done in most of the circumstances that are likely to arise in the average do-it-yourself project.

FUNCTION AND PURPOSE OF TILING

Why tile a surface in the first place? It is usually more expensive than paint or wallpaper, takes longer, is more difficult to do and the range of colours and patterns is little different from those available in other materials.

The reason is that tiles are very durable. They can resist knocks, abrasion and water, and can be used in situations where most other materials would quickly deteriorate. Ceramics are some of the most durable materials known to man and ceramic tiles can be counted on to last indefinitely without loosing the freshness of their appearance.

In both bathrooms and kitchens hygiene is important. Surfaces need to be cleaned regularly and thoroughly, often with abrasive chemical cleaners, without developing surface faults that could harbour bacteria. They also need to be hard and strong enough to withstand the day to day knocks which all such surfaces receive in commercial situations. Tiling can be the easiest way of providing a durable, easily cleaned surface, and commercially is often used just for these properties.

Tiles are most often used when a combination of durability and decoration is needed. Tile manufacturing techniques have evolved in a way that makes an enormous range of designs, textures and finishes available. Some of the technologies, such as stencilling and silk-screen printing, have been 'borrowed' from other trades. Others, like encaustic decoration and mosaic work, are unique to tiling and have evolved into high art forms in their own right. The range of tiles available today is huge and covers just about any imaginable situation from the point of view of beauty or practicality.

Lastly, but certainly not least, is the desirability factor. The expensive decorative forms of tiling have always presented an image of both prestige and opulence. It is only in the last fifty years or so that decorative tiles of any type have been affordable to most people. A century ago even the most basic form of tiling would have been beyond the means of the majority of the population. Modern computerized manufacturing methods, combined with new fixatives and fixing techniques, now make it possible for everyone to have the finishes that were once only available to the wealthiest in society.

BEFORE YOU START

Readers conversant with the building trade will probably notice that the technical terms used in this book do not necessarily coincide with the ones that they are used to. These do vary up and down the country and I have tried to use terms that are as descriptive of the situation as possible. Failing this, I have used the ones I was brought up with.

This book tries to tell the do-it-yourself tradesman not just how to tile, but the situations he or she should avoid. Readers are advised to read the whole book before starting work, because tiling is one of those trades where the processes constantly reflect

The right safety equipment is important.

back on earlier stages. You can create problems for yourself that you will not notice until a week later. Getting an idea of the whole process first will help to avoid those situations which every tiler gets into when first learning the trade.

Some of the processes described here are not strictly 'to the book'. This is deliberate as it reflects what actually happens on sites, rather than the hypothetical position that can sometimes be impractical.

With floor tiling there is no certain division between paving and tiling as the terms cover fields that overlap. Likewise, there is no strict dividing line between semi-structural faience cladding and ordinary wall tiling. For the purposes of this book a tile will be considered as a hard, inflexible, mineral-based facing which has to be bonded to a base or backing to give it the structural strength it needs.

HEALTH AND SAFETY

There is a great emphasis today on the safety aspects of building operations. The days have gone when the risks were usually mechanical and were restricted mainly to such things as hitting your thumb with a hammer or getting something in your eye. Materials today are more complex and potentially more dangerous: cement is faster reacting; adhesives and grouts are complex mixtures containing obscure resins; cutting equipment is often powered by electricity; and commercial power tools, originally intended for fully skilled tradesmen, can be hired by the general public. Safety should be the DIYer's top priority. There is little point in starting a job if you are not going to keep yourself in a condition to finish it.

There are a few dangers which are specific to the trade. The glaze on the surface of glazed tiles is really a layer of glass and is just as sharp. Raw edges and splinters are produced when tiles are being cut; these should always be handled carefully and waste disposed of safely. Porcelain and other vitrified tiles have this property through the whole of their thickness. Always take care when handling cut tiles and avoid touching freshly cut edges on tiles if you can. Always wear gloves when clearing debris away.

Some of the products used in tiling can occasionally result in an allergic reaction if you are exposed to them for too long. Some people go all their working lives with no problems. Do not count on being one of the lucky ones. If the instructions for the product say you should wear protective clothing, then do so.

The most common accidents in the building trade are those involving falls. Always make sure that you have a secure footing, particularly when working in awkward corners or at a height. You will usually be using both hands for the job in hand, and will have none to spare for an emergency.

All power tools have the potential to be dangerous. In the building trade power tools are 110V. Those intended for domestic or DIY use are usually 240V, which places you potentially at more risk than the professional. Use circuit breakers and always keep it in mind that water and electricity do not mix.

Whilst tiling is not the most hazardous activity in the building industry, accidents are always waiting to happen and you can never relax your guard. It is not possible, in a book of this length, to cover every conceivable safety issue in detail. However, here are a few useful tips:

- **Always expect that an accident will happen**. Because if you don't, it will. Accidents are only prevented by constantly taking precautions against them.
- **Always read the instructions**. They are not there just to decorate the bag or the box. When you have read them, *do as they say*.
- **Work tidily**. If it isn't needed for the job in hand, get it out of the way. There isn't a tiler alive who hasn't knelt on a nail in a piece of lathe he has left lying about.
- **Concentrate on the job in hand**. Most accidents happen when you try to do two things at once, like thinking about tomorrow night's date while using a bench saw that is powerful enough to throw you through a wall.
- **If the job calls for protective clothing, use it**. The gloves are *not* for keeping your hands warm and whilst goggles might not improve your eyesight, they might help you to keep it.
- **Make sure that you have the right gear**. If you are working 3m up a wall, a step stool with a few tile boxes on top is *not the right gear*.
- **Keep some variety in the work, don't do too much of anything at one time**. This may not seem like a health and safety tip, but doing too much of the same thing makes you careless of safety. Apart from that, spending all day doing nothing but cutting with tile nippers will give you an insight into that most fashionable of disorders – Repetitive Strain Injury.

DESIGN CONSIDERATIONS

Tiling is different from other forms of decoration. It is much more permanent, and if you get it wrong you are usually going to have to live with it for a long time. Form, texture and colour are always going to be down to personal taste. However, within any trade there are situations which are known to cause problems. If you know what the problem is, then you can either avoid it or work around it. The following few notes may help you to understand the potential pitfalls.

Permanence vs Fashion

Tiling is much more expensive and permanent than other forms of decoration. The more up to date and influenced by immediate fashion your choice is, the sooner it will look dated. If you are the kind of person who doesn't mind such things, or retiling every few years, that is fine, but if you consider tiling to be a 'once in a lifetime' event, a more classical design might be more appropriate than the latest trend.

Size

The size of the tiles has a considerable effect on the final appearance of the tiling. However, whether or not a tile looks too big or too small for an area will depend upon more than just the tile size. A contrasting grout colour, coloured edges or borders, or a design feature on the tile all tend to make the size of the tile more noticeable and the scheme fussier.

Tip

Take the time and trouble to finalize your design in detail before you start, then stick to it. Changing your mind can prove expensive.

A small amount of decorative feature can give a lift to an otherwise basic tile.

With low contrast colour schemes, such as plain white or cream tiles with white joints, tile size is not usually an issue. In such cases the consideration of size is usually purely practical.

Form

Shaped tiles make the setting out more critical and can be time-consuming to cut. This is particularly so for wall tiling, where there are usually more corners to be negotiated. If the tile is both small and has a complicated shape, true vertical and horizontal corners and a near perfect setting out are essential.

Tip

If you are using random decorative insert tiles, mark their approximate positions on the wall before you start tiling. You will then know that you are happy with their positions and can put the insert tiles in as you get to them. You will also know exactly how many insert tiles you need to buy.

Tile Colour

All the usual rules of interior decoration apply to tiles. Dark colours pull walls in and make rooms look smaller. Light colours have the opposite effect. Tile surfaces can be matt and rustic, or shiny and slick, decorative panels can be used to create features, inset strips and border tiles to create emphasis. All these points have to be considered and adjusted to your taste. The only thing to bear in mind is that tiling is permanent and not easy to alter, so take the time and trouble to get it right.

Grout Colour

Grout colour can have a considerable effect on the appearance of tiling, but coloured grouts can, occasionally, be difficult to handle or give problems. Some points to note are:

- **White on walls and grey on floors are the most usual grout colours**. They are the most tried and tested and the least subject to the vagaries of fashion.
- **Grey is, usually, the best colour for grouting floor tiles**. With a few special exceptions, the

joints will be slightly recessed and are going to go grey anyway as they collect traces of dirt. To watch them do so on a floor with white joints can be quite depressing. If you decide you must have white or a coloured grout on a floor, use one that will not discolour, such as an epoxy, and be prepared to scrub the joints clean on a regular basis.

- **Stick with proprietary coloured grouts**. You can mix your own colours, but a good colour match can be difficult to get right on a repeated basis.
- **Tiles can sometimes be stained by coloured grouts**. By the time you are grouting you have done most of the work. To have it spoiled at that stage is something you can do without. If in doubt, check with your supplier or do a test first.
- **Be careful if using high-contrast grout colours (for example, black tiles with white grout or vice versa)**. You will be surprised how little variation in joint width is needed to show up in

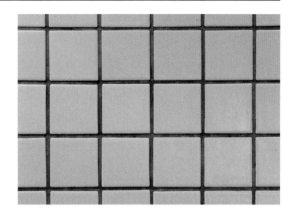

Accurate joints are essential if using a contrasting grout.

such cases. The quality of tiling has to be really high for it to look good. In extreme cases you won't know if the tiling was good enough until you have grouted it.

CHAPTER 1

Materials and Equipment

CHOOSING AND BUYING TILES

Tiles have to be capable of being fixed to a good standard on your particular job and of looking good in the long term, so it pays to be practical about choice. Once tiles are fixed, remedial work tends to be both messy and expensive. A few simple rules can help.

Can you handle the material and situation?
The cutting and fixing of certain materials can frighten people with a lifetime in the trade. If you have all the time and money in the world, that is fine, you will get over the problems eventually. If not, it pays to be honest with yourself and choose a tile you know you can handle.

Check that the tiles are suitable for the usage they are going to get.
The supplier does not want an unhappy customer. Tell them what you are using the tiles for and ask his opinion. Is the tile surface or glaze tough enough? Is the tile body strong enough? Are they easy to clean? There are plenty of questions to ask. Do not assume that any tile is suitable for any situation. Some wall tiles can be incredibly tough and some floor tiles are only suitable for the lightest traffic.

Be aware of the properties of the tile.
For example: some can be difficult to cut. You will need access to a diamond core drill if a neat hole in a porcelain tile is required. Large tiles will usually involve more waste than small ones. Smaller tiles are

OPPOSITE: Tiles are unmatched for putting a bit of drama into a bathroom or cloakroom.

RIGHT: Some tiles are more difficult to cut than others. Size, material and thickness all play a part.

not always the easiest to cut. You are going to need an electric saw for most jobs involving natural stones.

Such considerations may seem obvious, but it is surprising how easy it is to get carried away by a television programme that gives the impression that 20 square metres of marble tiles can be fixed in a couple of hours.

Is the material practical for the situation?
A job lot of 20mm thick marble tiles for the bathroom walls may be a bargain, but they will be heavy enough to pull the plaster off the wall and you will need a mortgage to pay for the equipment to cut them.

Is the size practical for the situation?
If all you have to tile is a small toilet floor with a lot of pipes through it, a large tile is not the best choice. Apart from the wastage you are likely to have, trying to cut a single, large tile neatly around three or four pipes of assorted sizes, plus part of a toilet base, is not easy, particularly in a tight corner.

Is the colour practical for the situation?
If you live on a working farm and have six dogs, you are unlikely to be happy with white floor tiles. The floor will, of course, look good on day one.

Make sure that you buy enough tiles for the job.
Tiles can vary in colour from batch to batch. You cannot blame the supplier if you need five or six tiles to finish a job and find that he cannot match the colour six months later. Ask if the problem could arise and, if it could, see if you can negotiate a 'sale or return' deal. At the very least, make sure that you have a note of all the tile details, including the batch and shade numbers. You should always try to have a few tiles left over to do the future repairs that will certainly arise if you don't have the tiles to do them.

MATERIALS

Tiles

Tiles today come in a huge range of forms and materials and the selection available is such that choice can

Tiles come in a huge range of types and sizes.

be difficult and sometimes confusing. From the tiler's point of view the consideration is practical. The tile has to be suitable for the job, both with regard to carrying out the work and the performance of the tiling afterwards. For example, there is little point in choosing tiles that you haven't the equipment to cut, or using a tile for flooring which is not strong enough to stand up to the particular situation.

Ceramic Tiles

Ceramic tiles come in two forms, glazed and unglazed. The glaze is a layer of glass fired onto the surface of the tile body. This gives the tile its colour and texture. An unglazed tile does not have a layer of glaze, the body of the tile providing the finished surface. The body of the tile can vary in hardness according to its constituents and the temperature at which it is fired. This can vary from being soft enough to carve with a penknife, to being harder and denser than glass.

As a general rule, any tile can be used on a wall, as all tiles will be strong enough for such a situation; the only other consideration is the ease of cleaning. However, for flooring work the tile has to be strong enough to take the loads and the wear and tear involved. Tiles should therefore be selected with the usage in mind. Today, there are many glazed tiles available for flooring, but it should always be borne in mind that the wearing surface is only as thick as the glaze, and if this wears through the body of the tile will show. Glazed floor tiles are usually classified according to their hardness and suitability for a particular situation. For very heavy or commercial use an unglazed tile should always be considered.

Frost resistance is essential for tiling out of doors. Water absorbed into the body of the tile can freeze and expand, causing the tile to break down. You must use tiles that are suitable for outside work and should never simply assume that a tile is suitable for external use. Tiles are classified for this purpose and the manufacturer's guidance should always be followed. If you are buying tiles for outside use always make this known to your supplier.

Natural Stone Tiles

Natural stone tiles are usually limestone, marble, slate or granite. In natural materials there is a huge range

Natural stones differ in more than just colour. The ones shown here vary greatly in hardness and ease of working.

of variability from the point of view of hardness, density, the tendency to stain and mark, and just about every other property you can think of. Limestone is amorphous and can be very soft and porous. Marble has a crystalline structure, is harder and is usually sold highly polished. Slate is dense, has quite a strong laminar structure, does not take a natural polish and can be difficult to maintain. Granite can be very hard and strong and takes a high polish. However, within these general categories there are huge variations. Some slates can mark very easily and all marbles can be damaged by quite mild acids. Some stones need to be sealed before fixing and some do not. All of these natural materials are difficult to cut compared to ceramic tiles and you will need an electric saw to do it effectively.

These materials are unmatched in their beauty and character, and these are the properties that have made them so desirable for the whole of history. The richness and colour that can be obtained cannot be matched by other finishes. But it can be a minefield. There are some 2,000 different marbles available commercially and new ones are appearing all the time. With all natural stones the goalposts are constantly being moved. As a quarry is worked the nature and quality of a stone can change for better or worse. It is a huge subject that is changing constantly and you should always ask the supplier's advice.

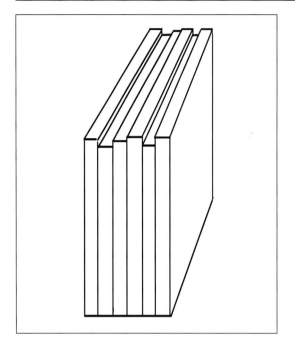

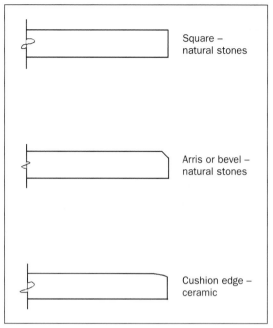

Stacking tiles on edge on a flat surface will show up any size variation.

Tile edge details.

SHAPE AND FORM

Sizes

The shapes and sizes that are available in tiles are greater now than they have ever been. New technology has enabled the manufacturers to produce tiles of a size that would have been unthinkable a few years ago. Tiles, like all ceramic products, tend to distort a little when fired and it is only relatively recently that it has been possible to produce large sizes while still keeping the tiles flat and square. Sizes can vary from 1cm square mosaic tiles up to panels that are too big to be considered as tiles and have to be mechanically fixed. Generally, the size of tile that you will be willing to handle will be dictated by the type of job you are doing and the equipment, particularly the cutting tools, that you have available.

Tolerances and Distortion

Tiles today usually have to meet strict standards and are usually quite accurate in size, but with handmade tiles it is still possible to have considerable size variation and distortion. This is not necessarily a problem, but it is important that you know about it before you start work. Tiles with large amounts of size variation or that are distorted in any way, will need to be fixed with wider joints to achieve a satisfactory end result.

To check tiles for size all that is necessary is to take a random sample of about ten or so tiles and hold these vertically, like a pack of cards on edge, on a flat smooth surface. Any size variation will immediately become apparent on the top edges. Holding two tiles face to face or placing tiles face down on a flat surface will usually show up any undue distortion.

Why the shape of the tile edge is important.
For the last fifty years or so practically all ceramic tiles have been produced with 'cushion edges'. This is a slight roll or curve to the front edges of the tile. The reason for this is that it can be very difficult to get tiles that have very square edges to look good under all light conditions, particularly if they are not flat.

By tending to throw any shadows into the joint, instead of onto the face of the next tile, a 'cushion edge' helps to hide any lipping of the tiles. If square-edged tiles are used, particularly with narrow joints, it is vital that the fixing is to a very high standard and that the tiles are as flat and free from distortion as possible.

The equivalent to this on a natural stone tile is the 'arrised' or bevelled edge. This is simply a slight angle (usually of about 45 degrees) ground onto the front edges of the tile during manufacture.

FIXATIVES

Adhesives are a subject where it pays to find out what the trade is using. The trade is always price conscious and cannot afford for things to go wrong. It doesn't matter how good the tiles are, if they drop off the wall you are not going to be happy. Adhesives fall into three categories, which are: Type C (Cementitious); Type D (Dispersion); Type R (Reaction resin).

All come in various types that have their own characteristic uses. These are:

Cement-Based Adhesives (Type C)

These are dry powders that need to be mixed with water and that set by hydration. They can be used for walls and floors in situations where traditionally sand and cement was used, and can be obtained in grey or white and in varieties for special situations (timber floors, rapid hardening, flexibility and so on). They are the best materials for wet situations as they are usually unaffected by water once they have set. Some can be mixed with additives to give additional properties, such as a degree of flexibility, higher bond strength and so on.

Combined Adhesive and Grout (Type D)

These adhesives are suitable for the smallest of jobs only, as they tend to be a compromise. The properties that you want in a grout are not necessarily those that you want in an adhesive and vice versa.

There is an adhesive available for just about any purpose you can think of.

Acrylic or PVA-Based General Purpose Adhesives (Type D)

This is a premixed material and is by far the most commonly used type of wall tiling adhesive. It sets by water loss as it dries out. It is easy to use (and to remove if it gets where it shouldn't), and is good for practically all wall tiling situations except where there is water or heat. The acrylic ones tend to have better antislip properties.

Water-Resistant Acrylic or PVA-Based General Purpose Adhesives (Type D)

Pretty much the same as above, but intended for situations where some water is present, for example domestic bathrooms and showers and so on. Please note that 'water resistant' is not the same as 'waterproof'. To get the meanings of these terms confused can invite disaster.

Two-Part Resin Adhesives (Type R)

These are two-part pre-measured materials, usually epoxy or polyester based. They are composed of the resin plus a hardener which have to be mixed on site. Two-part resin adhesives are usually materials for special or difficult situations. They are also usually much more expensive and generally more difficult to handle.

Sand and Cement

Not often used nowadays except for commercial flooring, a sand and cement mix is harder work, slower and more skill-demanding than adhesive fixing, but is still a good method of fixing tiles. For some specialist forms of tiling it is still the best method for high-quality work.

GROUTS

Grout is the material used to fill the joint between tiles. It is normally white or grey, but can be obtained in a variety of colours.

Premixed

Premixed grout comes in tubs ready to use, which has the advantage that there is less waste involved. However, it is expensive and is not generally used in the trade.

Grouts come in all sorts of types and colours.

Cement-Based Powder

This is mixed with water and is the traditional grouting material that still accounts for the vast majority of grout used. It is available in various types, some with special properties (rapid setting, flexibility, for wider joints and so on). A good range of colours is available.

Two-Part Resin

This usually consists of epoxide materials. Two-part resins are good for cleanability, chemical resistance and general toughness, but once they have set, practically nothing will remove them, so great care is needed in use. They are much more expensive than cement-based grouts and more difficult to use. They are not advisable for tiles with an 'open' or textured surface. Stick to ones that are water soluble until set.

TRIMS

Years ago tile manufacturers used to make a huge range of specially shaped tiles for all sorts of special applications. They sometimes had as many as ten or twelve different tiles just to get around corners. You could even get footrest tiles for showers and ashtray tiles for bathrooms.

Today, these have largely been replaced by purpose-made trims in plastic or metal. These are available in a huge range of sections for all sorts of purposes, such as getting around corners, step edging, decorative feature lines, providing water seals and so on. You name it, someone will be making a trim for it, probably in a large range of sizes and variations. To give you an idea of how big this field is, one of the major accessory manufacturers has over 3,000 lines.

These trims have taken a great deal of work out of the job and enable a DIY enthusiast to give a precision and cleanness of finish that would have been difficult for a professional tiler to match a few years ago. Whilst your local tile shop may only carry a basic range of corner trims in stock, if you need anything special, ask them. The range of available trims covers just about any situation you can imagine and will often be available on a twenty-four-hour delivery basis.

Today, there are trims for everything.

A plastic corner trim.

A step-edge trim.

A decorative insert trim.

Some manufacturers make external corner pieces.

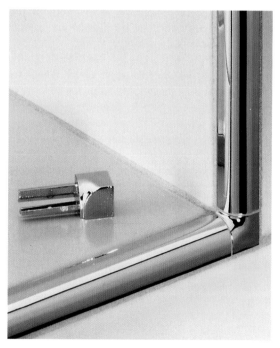

And even ones just for changing direction.

TOOLS

The range of tools available today is greater than it has ever been and the quality is generally excellent. Traditionally, it has always paid to buy the best quality that you can afford, on the basis that such tools will last longer. However, modern manufacturing systems have narrowed the quality gap and, unless you will have a continuous need for a tool, it is not always still the case today. This does not mean that buying poor-quality tools is sensible, only that it is now possible to buy decent quality tools at reasonable prices.

To find out which tools are best value, try to establish what the trade in your area is using. Tilers have to work both efficiently and to a price, and the tools they buy are usually the best value. Most trade tile suppliers stock a full range of tools for sale to the trade and are usually quite happy to sell to the general public.

Be practical about the purchase of tools. There is little point in paying for an expensive wet power saw if your tile supplier is prepared to cut your tiles for you for a quarter of the cost.

HAND TOOLS

A list of basic tools is given below. These are generally considered to be necessary to nearly any tiling job that is much larger than a splashback.

The range of tools available today is enormous compared to a few years ago and covers just about any eventuality.

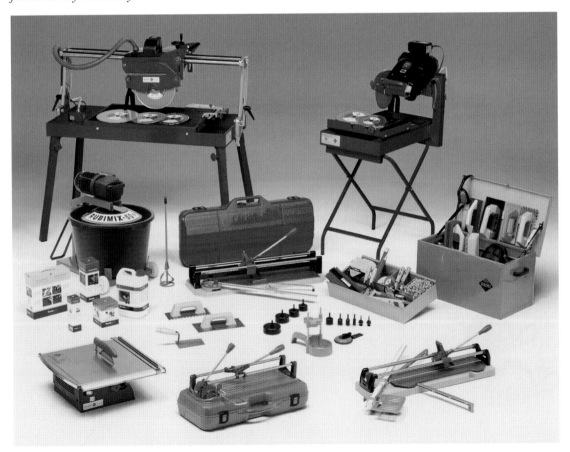

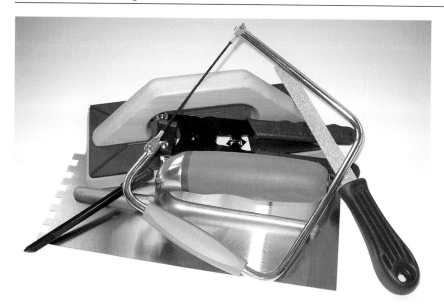

A few of the basic hand tools.

2m or 3m Steel Tape Measure

This is essential; if you have a larger project and can run to a 5m tape as well, so much the better.

Pencil

A pencil will be needed for marking natural stone, unglazed and matt glazed tiles, plaster and everything other than highly glazed tiles. For tiles with an absorbent surface, particularly natural stone tiles, never use anything else, as you may stain them.

Water-Based Felt-Tip Pen

Pencils will not easily mark a highly glazed tile. A felt-tip pen will, but make sure that it wipes off with a damp cloth. If you use it on plaster or unglazed tiles it won't last five minutes. A chinagraph pencil also works well.

Steel tape measures.

A water-based felt-tipped pen.

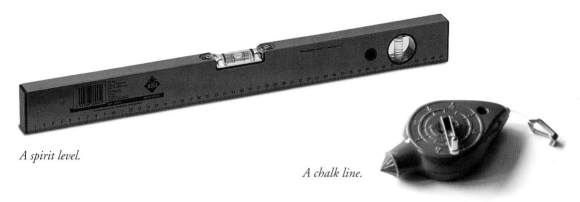

A spirit level.

A chalk line.

Plumb Line/Chalk Line

If you don't mind getting your hands dirty you can make a chalk line do both jobs. Try to get one with a natural fibre string. Some of the synthetic strings don't hold the chalk very well. Or you can just buy a ball of cotton string and make your own.

Spirit Level

A spirit level is the one thing where quality really counts. If this isn't accurate, you will have problems. As a rule, the longer the better, although a long one can be a nuisance in corners. A length of around 900mm is a good compromise. Make sure that you get one where the bubble is easily visible from both the side and above. Occasionally you find them where the bubble is only really visible from the side – this will drive you mad if you are working low down or on a floor.

Straight Edge

A straight edge consists of a straight piece of wood between 100mm and 200mm wide and about 20mm thick with parallel edges. It can either be bought or made from scrap timber. The length is normally between 2m and 2.5m *and it has to be straight.* A piece of blockboard is best, as it will not distort. If you are working in a small area you may need a short one as well. You can get expensive metal ones, but they are not necessary and they cannot easily be cut down.

Tip

To check a straight edge, lay it on a flat surface and use it to draw a fine line. Turn it over so that the same edge is on the line but with the other side uppermost. Any variation from the line indicates that the straight edge isn't.

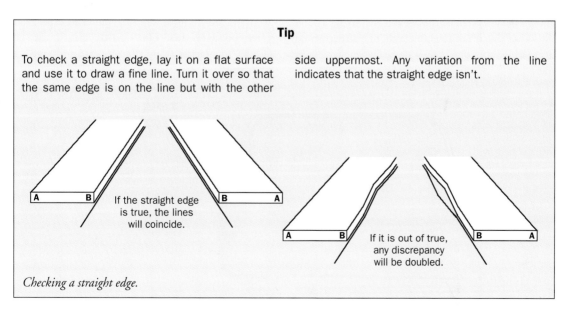

If the straight edge is true, the lines will coincide.

If it is out of true, any discrepancy will be doubled.

Checking a straight edge.

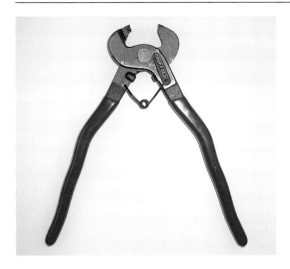

A tile scriber.

Tile nippers.

Tile Nippers

These are essential for small cuts, notching around things and adjusting cuts that didn't quite fit. You can also get them with small jaws set at an angle intended to get into tight corners. These are sometimes called 'parrot' or 'parrot-jawed' nippers.

Tile Scriber

A tile scriber scribes the tile face as part of the cutting process. A good-quality pencil-type glass cutter will also do the job on most tiles. If you are buying a hand tile cutter this is not essential, although a tiler would never be without one as they are fast when using light tiles.

A hand tile cutter.

Hand Tile Cutter

This is a combination tool that is really a tile breaker with a scribing wheel built in. These are great for general cutting of lighter tiles. A must!

Hand Tile Saw

This is basically a fretsaw for ceramics. It is useful for awkward cuts on most wall tiles, but don't expect too much on hard tiles. On vitrified tiles it can be quicker to practise using the nippers until you get really good.

A hand tile saw.

Tile File or a Coarse Abrasive Block

A tool for smoothing the cut edges of tiles and for taking out minor irregularities. A coarse emery cloth over a wooden former also works well. Sandpaper will not do. Whatever you use has to be tougher than the tile, and sandpaper isn't.

Gauging or Pointing Trowel

These are useful for 'buttering' (spreading) adhesive on the backs of tiles and lots of other things. The gauging trowel is larger than the pointing trowel and is more of a general-purpose tool. If you get seriously into tiling you will need both.

A Notched (Serrated) Floating Trowel or an Adhesive Spreader

These are for putting adhesive on the wall or floor to a consistent thickness. They come with various depth notches according to the situation and the adhesive

being used. A spreader is a smaller plastic or metal tool intended originally for the DIY market. It does the same job as the serrated float, though not as quickly or efficiently, but can be handy for small areas.

Rubber-Headed Hammer

Forget the glass nail joke! This is not essential, but has a decided advantage if you are going to do a lot of floor tiling, as it helps to prevent breakages.

Squeegee

Squeegees are for working grout into joints. They can consist of anything from a piece of stiff rubber

A serrated floating trowel.

A tile file.

A gauging trowel.

A rubber mallet or hammer.

Squeegees.

mounted onto a piece of wood or a purpose-made floating trowel with a soft face. Not essential for small work but a decided advantage.

Spacer pegs.

Sponge

A sponge is used for cleaning tiles off both before and after grouting. You will need cloths as well, but they cannot match a sponge for general cleaning. Get the cheapest you can as they don't last long. Alternatively, save up the ones that have become too grotty for the bathroom.

Spacer Pegs

These are usually bought when you purchase the tiles. They are small plastic inserts which go into the tile joints to keep the spacing correct until the adhesive has set. Sounds simple, but one manufacturer alone makes over forty different types and sizes. They are usually of three types: straight, wedge-shaped and cross-shaped. The wedge-shaped ones are for joints that you want to adjust. The cross-shaped ones were originally intended to fit into the corners where four tiles meet, but they do make it hard to adjust your tiles and are difficult to remove. As you shouldn't really leave anything in the joints that can interfere with the grout it is better just to stick one prong into the joint, leaving the others as convenient handles. Used like this, they are great on floors as they can't drop down into the joints. For the majority of walling work you will only need the straight ones.

ADVANCED AND POWER TOOLS

The sky is the limit when it comes to spending on these. However, today there is plenty of quite good equipment available at a reasonable price.

Laser Level

There are various types of laser levels on the market and they can now be purchased quite cheaply. They can save you a great deal of time but they are all slightly different, so take the time to choose one that suits you and learn how to use it properly. If the instructions are not brilliant, and they sometimes aren't, see if you know someone who can show you.

Bench-Type Tile Cutter

This tool and the electric saw have just about entirely replaced the old-fashioned cutting chisel and hammer for cutting floor tiles. Invaluable if you have a lot of tiles to cut. They come in all sorts of sizes and qualities, but some aspects are important to consider when purchasing one. Make sure you can get spare scribing wheels for it. It needs a bed long enough to take the longest cut you will need to make (and this can be greater than the stated tile size if you are cutting on the diagonal). Ensure that it is strong enough for the job, as some will struggle when cutting porcelain or quarry tiles.

Electric Bench Saw

This is probably the ultimate for the do-it-yourselfer, and is pretty near essential if you have any quantity of natural stone tiles to cut. For a small job it may be cheaper to mark up the tiles and get your supplier to cut them; most good specialist suppliers will offer this service. As with all bench cutters make sure that you can get spare blades and that the bed is long enough for the tile.

A bench tile cutter.

A laser level.

An electric bench saw.

CHAPTER 2

Cutting

The term 'cutting' with regard to tiles is a misnomer because the only time a tile is truly being cut is when a saw, mechanical or manual, is being used. In the large majority of cases, what is being achieved is a controlled break. The intention is to create a line of weakness on which the tile can be made to break as cleanly and evenly as possible. This is done by using a tile scriber or the hardened wheel of a tile cutter to scribe a line into the face of the tile and then to exert pressure until the tile breaks.

There is a huge variation in the ease with which tiles can be cut. Generally, the thicker and harder a tile is, the more difficult it will be. However, other factors, such as the temperature the tiles were fired at, and the consistency of the tile body, will all play a part.

With modern equipment you are not likely to have any serious difficulties.

If in any doubt at all, just ask your tile supplier "What are they like to cut?" It might seem a silly question but it is quite normal in the trade, and could save you a lot of aggravation.

THE MATERIALS

Glazed Tiles

These are usually the easiest to cut. The glaze forms a convenient layer in which to create a line of weakness. There are some glazed tiles with highly vitrified bodies that can be more difficult, as can some porcelain tiles.

OPPOSITE: Pastel colours add a softness to a colour scheme.

Unglazed Tiles

Unglazed tiles are not the problem that they used to be. Modern tiles usually have a very consistent body and cut readily with modern equipment. The sheer hardness and toughness of thicker tiles can be quite hard on both hands and tools. If you are laying anything like an industrial quarry tile you will need quite heavy cutting gear.

Natural Stone Tiles

There is a huge variability in hardness and all are difficult to cut compared to ceramics. An electric saw is essential. Make sure that your supplier offers a cutting service as even professional tilers will prefer to have tiles cut for them at times. Before you are committed to using the tiles, check what they charge for cutting, as it can add substantially to the final bill.

Tiles, compared to many DIY materials, are time-consuming to cut and it cannot be emphasised too much how important accurate measuring is. Take the time and trouble to get it right. If you have doubts or a really difficult cut, make a template. It is easier to spend five minutes making a template than it is to have to redo a cut which takes half an hour.

CUTTING TECHNIQUES

Straight Cutting

Straight cutting in light tiles is quite a simple operation. Once the tile has been marked, place it face up on a firm surface. Using a metal ruler (or another tile), scribe a clean line into the glaze using either a tile scriber or a good glass cutter. Place a support under each end of the scribe and in line with it.

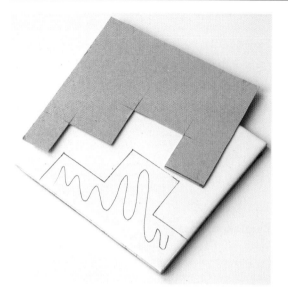

Make a template if you have any doubts about being able to mark a cut accurately.

Tip

Rules and straight edges have a habit of sliding about when you are scribing shiny glazed tiles. A strip of self-adhesive rubber of the type used as draft excluder stuck on the rule can help to keep it in position.

(Matchsticks will do when you first try it. You will use a short, thin straight edge as you speed up.) Press down firmly and evenly on each side of the tile and it will break cleanly on the line.

All other tile cutters working on the 'scribe and break' method use the same principle of forming a line of weakness and then exerting force until the tile breaks. With a hand tile cutter the tile is scribed using the built-in cutting wheel and then placed between the jaws with the scribed face uppermost.

The top jaw has two flat flanges which exert pressure evenly to the tile on each side of the scribe line. The lower jaw is a single narrow metal bar which does the same thing directly below the scribe and in line with it. Pressure on the handles will cause the tile to break on the line.

Using a bench-type cutter, the tile is laid, face up, flat on the bed of the cutter. A handle that moves on rails has a replaceable cutting wheel attached to it. The cutting wheel is lined up over your line and the wheel pushed across the surface of the tile whilst exerting an even, light, downward pressure on the handle. Once the scribe is complete, a downward movement of the handle brings two flanges into play that press the tile down onto a ridge in the bed

Tip

When scribing tiles, aim to do it in *one* clean movement, going over the line repeatedly makes the tile less likely to break cleanly.

Scribing a cut.

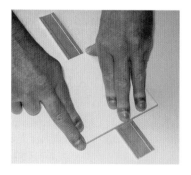

Place support under the line and press down on each side.

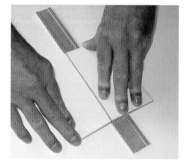

The tile should break cleanly.

Scribing with a hand tile cutter.

The cutter will split the tile with little effort.

of the cutter, which breaks the tile on the scribed line. There are many variations on this theme, but generally they all work on the same principle.

Using Tile Nippers

This is the one tool where practice does pay. Although slow, with practice it is possible to do complex cuts that are hard to match by any other method. As with the other cutters, what we are trying to achieve is a controlled break, or in this case a series of controlled breaks.

Until you have worked up a degree of expertise with nippers it pays to scribe the tile first, as you would for any other cut, as it helps to achieve a neat line. The technique is then to hold the tile in one hand, face up. The edge of the tile is placed between the jaws of the cutter and the handles squeezed whilst making a slight downward twisting movement of the wrist. A piece of the tile will break off on the line of the jaw with the break running to the edge of the tile. This process is repeated until the desired line is reached.

If forming a notch in a tile you work alternately from each side and the last bit is removed from the internal corner with the file or abrasive block.

The piece of tile you are removing will always

> **Tip**
>
> If you have a difficult cut and are using a hand cutter, exert pressure until you see the cut start to 'run' (the scribe line starts to open), then turn the tile around and finish it from the other end of the scribe line. With practice, it is possible to cut a quadrant out of a light tile.

A good bench tile cutter is both fast and accurate and is great for repetitive cuts.

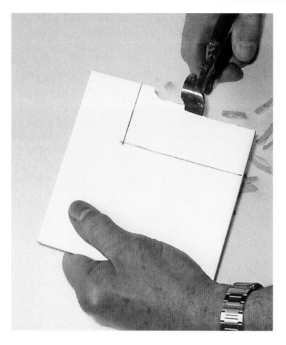

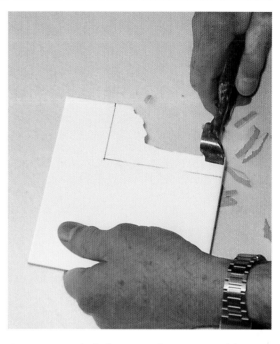

Start by nibbling in from the edge. Keep away from the lines to start with.

Progress towards the lines. Until you gain confidence only remove small pieces at a time.

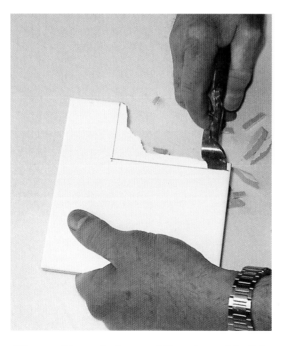

When working to the line, work from the outside of the tile towards the corner.

Clean out the corner carefully. Use a tile file if necessary.

break on the line of least resistance and you should try to keep this in the waste section of the tile. The easiest way to do this is to stick to the principle of 'little and often'. Trying to take out too much at one time is the surest way of breaking tiles.

Sawing

Hand sawing tiles can be slow, but produces a good finish and gives an easy way of doing small radius internal curves which are difficult by other means. The use of the saw is self-evident. As with all saws, don't use too much force. With thin, light tiles or awkwardly shaped cuts the force of the saw will sometimes cause the tile to break. It can be useful to place a piece of plywood or MDF under the tile and then to cut through both the tile and the board. It will not make much difference to the saw and the board will usually give enough support to stop the tile breaking.

Notching

You will probably spend as much time notching tiles as you will in doing all the other cutting put together, so any time savings are worth having. You will develop your own favourite system. Notching with nippers is the most usual method. Another way is to saw the shorter leg of the notch and then to scribe the other leg and break off the waste. An electric saw is the easiest way and can make this quite a fast operation.

Split and Notch

Split and notch is the traditional and most common way of cutting around pipes and brackets. The tile is first cut into two pieces on the centre line of the pipe. Each half of the tile is then notched around the obstruction and the tile is put back together as one unit when it is fixed. Properly and carefully done with the cut grouted to match the tile, it can make a very tidy finish.

Drilling

If the plumbing has been 'first fixed', that is, all the pipes are in position but the sink, W.C. and so on have not yet been fitted, it is possible to pre-drill a tile to fit around a pipe. It does call for the tiles being very accurately marked if you want a really good

Split.

Notch.

Finished split and notched cut.

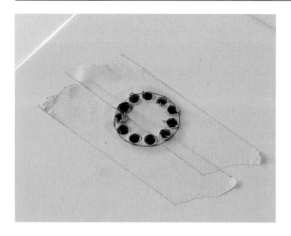

A 'stitch drilled' hole. Note the masking tape.

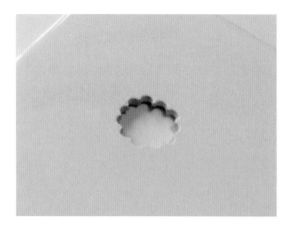

With the centre removed.

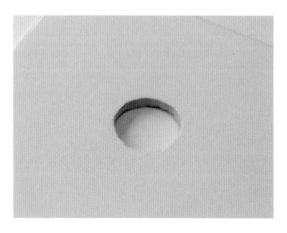

After cleaning up.

> **Tip**
>
> Always stick masking tape on a tile you are going to drill. It stops the drill bit slipping and any pen or pencil marks peel off with the tape.

finish. Drilling is best done in a wet drill stand using a diamond core bit with the tile fully supported on a flat piece of board. For some high-quality porcelain tiles this is practically the only way they can be drilled. Unfortunately, this is not equipment that the average DIY person is likely to have access to, but some tile suppliers will do it for you if you have marked the tiles up.

It can also be done, albeit more slowly, by 'stitch' drilling the tile using a good masonry bit. This involves drilling a series of holes close together around the perimeter in the waste material of the

You can buy drilling attachments as 'add-ons' to some bench cutters.

marked hole. A few more are then drilled in the waste material until it is weak enough to be broken out. The edge of the hole is then tidied up using a half round file or a rolled piece of coarse emery cloth wrapped around a piece of dowel.

Another alternative is to use one of the drilling attachments that can be bought as 'add-ons' to some of the bench-type tile cutters.

Power Machine Cutting

There is such a range of electric power tools available that it is impossible to give more than general advice.

All machines of this type cut by abrasion. The abrasive wheels that do the cutting are usually made from steel with diamond cutting edges.

The lighter type of electric saw is built on very similar lines to a small bench saw. The main difference is that it has a water bath in which the lower half of the blade runs. This is to provide lubrication for the cutting process and to keep the blade from overheating. Some of these can be quite reasonably priced.

The heavier types, usually intended for commercial use, have the blade mounted on an arm which is

A light wet electric tile saw. The cutting wheel is fixed and you push the tile against it.

A heavier type of wet electric tile saw. On this one the tile is stationary and the cutting wheel is moved across it.

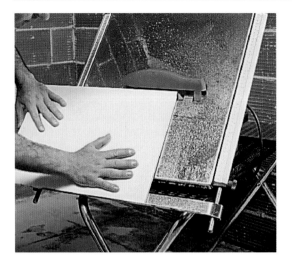

Some tile cutters allow mitre cutting.

With care and practice, more complicated cuts are possible with some saws.

pulled across the tile. Water is sprayed onto the blade as it cuts. On some cutters the tile is held on a wheeled bed that can be moved to and fro under the cutting wheel, which is brought down onto the face of the tile.

All electric machines are expensive compared with hand tools, but you may be able to hire one. If you do decide to buy one rather than hire, make sure that you will be able to get spares. With all power tools always follow the manufacturer's instructions to the letter. A machine that is capable of cutting a hard ceramic tile in half will have no trouble doing the same to your fingers.

CHAPTER 3

Wall Tiling

GETTING THE JOB READY

Any work necessary to the fixtures and fittings in a room should be carried out before the tiling commences. Strip out the room properly. Take down redundant items before you start the tiling, not when you get up to them. You do not need to find out at the last minute that there is no plaster behind that old cupboard in the corner.

On new work it is usual for a tiler to do his work after the plumber's 'first fix' but before his 'second fix', that is, after all the pipes are in, but before toilet and sink and so on are fitted. This creates a neater finish and avoids lots of difficult cutting. The exceptions to this are things that have to be tiled in, such as baths, shower trays, kitchen worktops and the like.

It will not always be possible for you to work like this, but if you can it is ideal. Taking a pedestal sink or a W.C. out is not a huge job, particularly if shut-off valves have been fitted to the pipes, but bear in mind that the thickness of the tiles will change the position of the sink or W.C. when you come to put them back, and some plumbing adjustments may be required. However, in these days of flexible connectors this is not always as difficult as it used to be. Make sure that anything that is going to be tiled around is secure and rigid and is in the right place. Once you have tiled it in, a wobbly or badly positioned bath will cause problems out of all proportion to the amount of effort that would have been needed to remedy it in the first place. Baths, shower trays, kitchen worktops and so on should be in such a

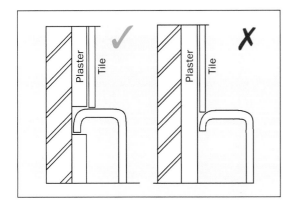

Try to ensure that tiles fit down onto to a bath or shower tray. A tile face behind the 'roll' on a bath leaves a place for water to gather and is difficult to seal.

A jointing trim to a bath. This one is more flexible than most. Here it has been used in conjunction with a waterproofing membrane to the wall.

Always try to fix tiles under the final lighting conditions. This shows the effect of two different lighting conditions on the same wall tiling.

position that the tiles can sit squarely down onto a horizontal surface.

One of the problems associated with tiling is the provision of an adequate water seal down to horizontal surfaces where water is going to lie, such as the edges of baths and shower trays. Where possible, it is always better to have the tiles fitted square down onto these, and the joint sealed with silicone rubber sealant or a purpose-made trim. The 'sit-on' plastic trims have a horizontal leg which sits onto the edge of the bath and a vertical one which fits behind the bottom tile. The idea is that any water that runs down the face of the tiles has to run down into the bath or shower tray.

A good tight cut is not always possible if the bath is not perfectly positioned. In such a situation try not to leave a dip where water can gather – suitable

OPPOSITE: Although even lighting is usually the most flattering to tiling, a properly used spotlight can have a tremendous effect on a tile with a contoured face.

'sit-on' trims can help to cover the dip caused by the roll of a bath edge and are a vast improvement on the old method of covering the gap with a tile angle bead. They can also accommodate some movement of the bath.

Lighting

Lighting can have a huge effect on the apparent quality of the finished tiling. Try to arrange it that the lighting you use when you tile is as close to the final lighting as possible. This is particularly important if you are using wall or pelmet lights which are going to throw light on the wall at a narrow angle.

MOVEMENT AND MOVEMENT JOINTS

See if you are going to need any movement joints. We have all listened to our houses creak as they cool down after a hot day. When buildings are new they move as they dry out, and they never stop moving with temperature and atmospheric moisture. It is

A good range of movement joint trims are available for use in both walls and floors.

normal to make some provision for movement. To do this it is usual to put in some flexible joints that allow the movement to take place without damaging the tiles. At their most basic, movement joints are simply joints that have been filled with flexible sealant. The sealant is there to provide a cleanable filler which will deform, rather than crack and come loose, if movement does occur.

In commercial work being done to British Standards, however, this can become a complicated subject involving long calculations. Most domestic situations do not call for elaborate provision for movement, but common sense should prevail and movement joints should be incorporated where movement is obviously going to occur. This will usually take one of the following forms:

- Where the tiling meets another material such as a bath or a timber or metal finish.
- Where differing materials have differing moisture and thermal movement characteristics and will move with changes of temperature and/or

humidity. Baths and shower trays will also move as they take the weight of the bather and the water. Ordinary grouts are quite brittle and often crack and become loose in such situations. It is the usual practice to create a flexible joint by forming a fillet of flexible mastic. Today this is nearly always a silicone rubber. This material is very flexible, adheres very well, is easy to clean and relatively easy to apply. It is also reasonably easy to replace should the need arise.

- At any point where movement, no matter how small, could result in water getting behind the tiles. All buildings are continuously moving slightly and some cracks can be too small to see. Usually this is not a problem but it can give difficulties in very wet situations. As a precaution it is a good idea to run a fillet of silicone rubber in vulnerable situations such as the internal corners of the tiling in a shower, or anywhere that water can stand.
- Where there is a joint in the backing that is expected to move. This one is common sense. Just occasionally a builder will incorporate a movement joint in a wall. It will be there for a reason. This has to be brought through the tiling and a flexible joint formed. If you tile over it the chances are that the tiles will either crack or become loose.
- Where a large expanse of tiling can result in damage either from the expansion of the tiles or contraction of the backing.

Stress can build up between the backing and the tiling due to the expansion of the tiles, shrinkage of the backing, or a combination of both. This can result in tiles coming loose or cracking. To minimize the risk of this happening it is normal to break the tiling down into areas too small for the stress to accumulate to a degree where it will cause trouble. There is no set formula for this, but, providing the backing is sound and dry, they are not usually necessary on walls up to 2m or 3m long. Above that it does no harm to have a joint at any internal corner with another wall. If you have walls over 5m or 6m long then think about intermediate joints. These should be at 3m to 4.5m centres and evenly spaced down the length of the wall.

The forming of the joint is simply a matter of

creating a joint 5mm or 6mm wide that is kept free of adhesive and grout and filled with flexible filler, again silicone being the most common. Alternatively, a proprietary plastic extrusion can be incorporated in the tiling.

BACKINGS

Quite simply, the backing is the surface to which you are going to stick your tiles. The importance of the backing cannot be over emphasized. It does not matter how good the tiles are or how strong the adhesive is, if the backing is not sound, all or part of it can come away and bring the tiles with it.

The properties you want out of a backing are:

- **Suitability** It has to be suitable for the situation and the tiles that are going on it. If it is going to get wet then plasterboard or a timber-based material is not going to last long. If there is any chance of water getting through to the backing consider changing it to one that is unaffected by water. For situations that may be permanently wet such as shower trays and plunge baths then both the backing and the adhesive *must* be totally unaffected by water.
- **Stability** It shouldn't shrink or expand too much with changes in temperature or humidity.
- **Strength** It has to be strong enough to carry the weight of the tiles. Plaster and skimmed plasterboard are not always suitable for the heaviest tiles.
- **Flatness** It has to be flat enough to take the tiles without you having to thicken the bed too much. If it isn't, it has to be straightened up *before* you start tiling.
- **Cleanliness** It has to be clean and free from any loose or friable material. There is little point in sticking your tiles to a layer of loose paint or dust.

Types

Most backings fall into one of the following categories:

- **Structural** When the backing is part of the structure of the building, usually brickwork, blockwork or concrete. Although there is no technical reason why you cannot fix direct to these they are usually not flat enough, and the slightest movement in them can cause problems with the tiling.
- **In Situ Finishes** These are materials applied wet to a wall to bring it into line and to provide a finish. Plaster or sand and cement rendering are the most common. A good, sound plaster is one of the best backings. For wet situations or for outside work, a sand and cement render is better, as it will not soften or disintegrate if it gets wet. If the finish has not yet been applied and you have a choice, go for rendering if it is a wet situation.
- **Preformed Backings** These consist of plasterboard in its various forms, blockboard, chipboard and the thousand and one other proprietary materials that come in sheet form and can be dry fixed. These are becoming increasingly common on modern houses as part of the partitioning systems used to form the internal walls. Boards manufactured from cement are now widely available. Unlike plaster- or timber-based boards, these are unaffected by water and should be used wherever there is a danger of water getting through to the backing.

It is also possible to get sheet materials specifically designed as backings for tiling. These come in various thicknesses, some of them thick enough (50mm) to be used for semi-structural use. They have the advantage that they are unaffected by water and provide a more stable backing than the majority of the timber or plaster-based materials that are available. They are a definite advantage in wet situations such as showers.

These boards, together with the fixing systems that sometimes come with them, provide a good method of preparing a room to receive tiling without the need for wet finishes such as render or plaster. Providing the structure is adequate, the fixing systems available also enable a wall to be prepared to receive tiling even if the existing finish is unsound and/or the wall is badly out of line.

All preformed backings have the advantage that there is no waiting time for them to cure and dry out as there is with plaster or render.

PREPARATION

Together with setting out, preparation tends to be one of the things that is neglected, mainly because there appears to be so little return for the effort involved. The professional tiler knows, usually by painful experience, that if he doesn't put the effort into the preparation, he is going to have to put even more in later.

Checking the Backings

The first thing to do is to check that the backing is sound enough to take the weight of the tiling. Plaster or sand and cement render onto solid walls can be checked by tapping with anything hard such as a coin or a key. You will soon find out if any is loose, as it will have a distinctly hollow sound. Don't panic if there is some hollowness – it would be an unusual wall that didn't have any. But if it covers more than a small area, cut a hole in the plaster and see if the plaster comes away easily. If it does, then you are better off replacing it.

Plaster onto plasterboard doesn't usually present problems, as it is only a skim coat (a thin layer of finishing plaster). It is rare for it to become loose and is very obvious if it does. Timber based boards are best avoided if possible, as they tend to distort with moisture. In any event they need to be particularly well fixed and try not to have to fix tiles across joints in the board if you can avoid it.

Plasterboard, finished with a skim coat or not, plywood, blockboard, chipboard and all proprietary boards need to be checked for security and rigidity. They should be well supported at 300mm to 400mm centres (spacings) and there should be battens or noggins behind all the sheet edges. With the exception of plasterboard, the fixings should be screws, not nails, and, ideally, should be at not more than 350mm centres. The edges of all sheets should be solidly fixed and all screw heads should be flush with, or slightly below the surface of the board.

A simple test is to place all your fingertips against the wall and push firmly whilst leaning with your weight onto the wall. There should be little, if any, movement of the boards.

Preparing the Surface

Ensuring that the surface is clean is very important. Sticking the tiles to a layer of dust or dirt is not what we are trying to do. New surfaces will need little other than wiping down. Surfaces that have been painted will need rubbing over with a coarse abrasive paper to remove all loose paint. Whilst this needs to be done thoroughly, not every little bit of paint needs to be removed. The object is to remove anything that may come loose later. Some emulsion paints can blister and peel if they are wet for long enough and these need to be removed, but if paint is very well bonded then it should not present a problem. However, all painted surfaces should be well scored and scratched.

Once you are happy that the walls are as sound and clean as you can get them the next stage is to see what, if any, priming is required. The purpose of a primer is to reduce the porosity of the backing and to prevent it absorbing too much moisture and/or resin from the adhesive. The rule here is to check what the adhesive requires. The adhesive manufacturer will usually give recommendations for priming. A polymer modified cement-based adhesive, for example, will usually need a primer. A primer can also be used to bind a surface that is dusting or friable.

Occasionally you may find a plaster wall where the plasterer has done too good a job and 'over-trowelled' the wall. This only means that he has done such a good job that the plaster is very dense and takes on a shiny finish. In this case, simply go over it over with a fine sandpaper to break the surface before you fix the tiles.

If you are tiling onto new walls give them plenty of time to dry. In situ finishes have to be really dry before you fix tiles to them. They shrink as they dry out and you do not want them to do any shrinking after your tiles have been fixed. Give them as long as you can to dry; new plaster needs a minimum of four weeks to dry out and develop its full strength.

Tip

You will get a stronger bond onto bare plasterboard than you will to one that has been skimmed. As a guide, don't fix ceramic tiles thicker than 12mm onto bare plasterboard, 8mm if it has been skimmed. The tiles should be even thinner if you are using natural stones, which are heavier.

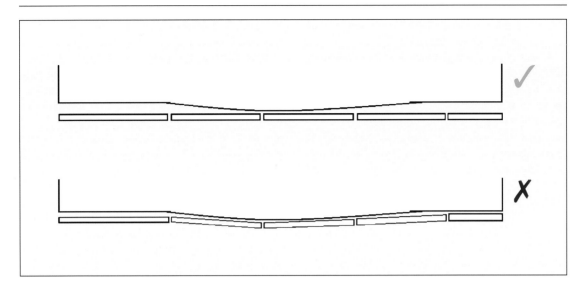

It is important to know the proudest point of a wall if you want your tiling to be flat and without lips.

Correcting Deviations – Is the Wall Flat Enough?

One of the most common problems that a tiler comes across is that of the walls not being flat enough to take the tiling. It is vital that you check the walls and know just how flat they are. In particular, you need to know where the proudest area is (the bit that sticks out the most). This is the area that will dictate the line to which you will have to work. The reason for this is that the tiling has to be on a line that allows you to fix the tiles true and straight. Tiling can be a series of flat planes but cannot follow a two-directional curve. If you start your tiling in a hollow part of the wall, you will have to follow the line of the wall as it comes forward and this will create a 'belly' on the tiling. As tiles are flat and you are creating a slight curve, the tiles will start to form lips and you will find it nearly impossible to produce a good job. The only option will be to take the tiles down and start again on a new line.

Years ago, checking a large wall involved doing complicated things with straight edges, plumb and string lines. Today, a cheap laser level can be used as a straight edge of infinite length which enables any length of wall to be checked quite quickly.

If the proud area is small and the wall surface is plaster it may be easier simply to cut the surface of the plaster back to a true line. However, in most cases it will involve bringing the wall to line.

It is not possible to give definitive figures on how far a wall has to be out of line before it needs correcting, as this varies with other factors, such as the tile size and the extent of the area that needs attention. For guidance, if it would mean increasing the bed thickness to more than the maximum recommended by the adhesive manufacturer for more than a very small part of the area involved, then consider correcting it before you start tiling.

If the deviation is not great this can be done by thickening the adhesive slightly as you go along. This is quite normal, but if done incorrectly it can give rise to problems and these are discussed later in the fixing section. Bear in mind that the smaller the tile, the flatter the backing needs to be. Trying to correct the line of the wall by thickening the bed when using very small tiles is difficult and can be impossible.

If the wall deviates by an amount that cannot be corrected in the fixing then there are various options. For small areas where there is not much deviation, a skim of adhesive will usually suffice. Fill in the hollow area with the adhesive using a trowel and then rule off the surface using a straight edge held tight against the wall. You do not need to trowel it smooth; it only needs to be flat. What is important is that it is allowed to dry thoroughly (and this means dry, not just set) before you tile onto it.

Where there is a large amount of deviation then different techniques are called for. For in situ finishes such as plaster or render, it may be as quick to cut out small areas and make them good. If you are not confident with plastering skills don't let it worry you, you need a flat wall not a smooth one. Once the old finish has been cut out, filling in and ruling off with a straight edge will usually be sufficient; if you are using sand and cement and it is very thick you may need to use more than one coat. If you do, let them dry properly between coats. For plastered walls there are many excellent one-coat plasters intended for such situations. Remember to damp the wall before you reapply render or plaster, as it will not stick to a dry surface. If in doubt, use a bonding agent on the wall first.

Walls faced with plasterboard or other wall boards are not as likely to be out of line as an in situ finish is, but it does happen. If they are badly out, then replacing or refixing the boards after packing them out to the correct line is the only real option, but, if you have the thickness available, you can overlay the existing backing with a new layer of board brought out to the correct line.

For walls that are simply too bad to tile, you will either have to replace the finish, or if you have the thickness to do it, overlay it with suitable board. In such situations the backing boards specifically made for tiling can save considerable time and effort and provide a good stable base.

CHAPTER 4

Making the Decisions

CHOOSING A TILE

Never make assumptions about what a tile is suitable for. Never use a tile sold for use on walls as a floor tile unless you know for certain that it will do the job. Most wall tiles simply do not have the strength needed for flooring use and the glaze might not be hard enough or non-slip enough either. As a general rule it is fine to use a floor tile on a wall, but floor tiles are often harder to cut and you usually get more cutting to do on wall tiling than you do on flooring. Unglazed floor tiles used on walls can have a pleasant rustic appearance, but bear in mind that they will also be more difficult to keep clean.

If using a heavy tile, make sure that the backing is going to be able to take the weight.

Mosaic tiles are small tiles that are usually fixed in sheet form rather than individually. Fixed this way, they are not as difficult to handle as might be imagined, but the walls do have to be flat and true. With large tiles it is possible to straighten a wall up as you go along, at least to some degree. You cannot do this with sheet materials like mosaic. This might not seem important, but with small tiles there are going to be a

Mosaic can be a very effective finish and can be used to add texture to a room without heavy design features or a lot of colour.

lot of joints. If the wall isn't reasonably flat the joints will 'wander' (they will not form a straight line) and will make any waviness very obvious. If you have any doubts, ask the supplier.

CHOOSING A FIXING METHOD

Adhesives

A little background information on the types of adhesive available may be of help here.

Tile adhesives fall into three main categories. The first are those that are intended for dry situations only. These are premixed materials, which normally come in a drum or a bucket and are one of the types technically known as 'dispersion' adhesives. They are economic and have good bond strength, but they are not suitable for wet areas, as they will soften quite readily if they become wet for any length of time. They are normally the cheapest adhesives available.

The second are the 'water-resistant' types. These are usually variants on the first type with additives that will give some resistance to water. They are often used in domestic showers and bathrooms. It is important that water is not allowed to penetrate the tiling, as most will not resist water forever, and if wet for long enough will eventually deteriorate.

The third type are the 'cementitious' waterproof adhesives. These are usually cement-based, need to be mixed with water on site and are unaffected by water once they have set. These are the ones used in areas that are permanently wet or rarely get chance to dry out properly. These adhesives are also available in special forms with characteristics such as rapid hardening or flexibility. Some can also have their properties altered with additives to give more flexibility or stronger adhesion.

There is a fourth type of adhesive. These are the epoxy or polyester two-part adhesives that sometimes combine the function of both adhesive and grout. These are mainly intended for industrial use where very high bond strength or some other special property such as chemical resistance is required. The only domestic situation in which these materials are likely to be needed is when they are used as grouts. They give a high level of resistance to oils and acids when used on kitchen worktops and they are occasionally used to give a greater degree of water resistance in abnormal situations.

It is very important to understand that the terms 'water resistant' and 'waterproof' do not mean that they will give these properties to your tiling job. It only means that the adhesive itself will resist water or will be unaffected by it. If you have fixed tiles onto plaster or plasterboard, and water gets through to that, the adhesive might not be affected by the water but the backing will be.

The things that dictate which fixative you are going to use are:

• The backing that you will be fixing to.
• The use to which the room is being put.

In a kitchen, unless there are any special circumstances, then a ready-mixed standard tile adhesive is going to be the most usual choice as it is both easy to use and economical. For a bathroom, a water-resistant product should always be used, even in areas that may not seem to be vulnerable. For wet areas, such as around baths, showers and so on, again a water-resistant material is necessary but using a 'solid bed' fixing technique. This, combined with proper use of silicone sealant, can help to prevent water coming into contact with the backing.

In areas that are subject to a great deal of water and get little chance to dry out, such as a sports club showers (or household with teenage daughters), then the use of both a waterproof adhesive *and* a waterproof backing has to be seriously considered. In such places there is always going to be a danger of some water getting through the tiles. If this does happen it is important that neither the adhesive nor the backing will be affected by it.

If you do have an existing backing which needs to be waterproofed, a relatively recent innovation is a waterproofing membrane that can be stuck to the wall before the tiles are fixed. This consists of an impervious polyethylene sheet manufactured in such

OPPOSITE: Classic designs needn't be dull or unfashionable. This one is influenced by the designs of Charles Rennie Mackintosh, which were the latest thing a hundred years ago.

a way that both sides provide a key for tile adhesive. It is fixed to the wall first with a suitable tile adhesive, the joints between the sheets being covered in a strip of the same material. The tiles are then fixed directly over the top of the sheeting. The idea is to provide an impervious layer sandwiched between two layers of waterproof tile adhesive, which will then prevent water getting through to the backing. The same material can also be used on floors.

As with all proprietary materials the manufacturer's instructions should be closely followed, as the effectiveness of the material depends upon it being applied properly, and water has a nasty habit showing up any trace of carelessness.

Grouts

These come in a large range of colours and types for different widths of joint. Some manufacturers do produce special ranges of flexible water-resistant grouts, but these can be difficult to find. Separate additives are sometimes available to give the grout more flexibility and water resistance. It is possible to get rapid-hardening grout, too, but colours are limited, and, for domestic situations, it has limited applications.

For the majority of tiling work, the standard cement-based grouts are going to be perfectly adequate. In a wet area, a flexible grout with increased water resistance can be good from the point of view of maintenance, and an epoxy grout is an advantage when tiling kitchen worktops. Another situation where an epoxy grout can be an advantage is where there is going to be a particularly aggressive situation, such as a power shower playing directly onto a wall, as this can be quite hard on the grouting.

However, do bear in mind that the trade survived for most of its history without these specialized products and they do add cost. If you are on a tight budget, consider whether or not an advantage is really a necessity.

If a coloured grout is required try to bear in mind the obvious stumbling blocks:

- Stick with proprietary brands.
- Check with the supplier regarding the chance of the tiles staining. If you have any doubts at all do a test before you commit yourself.
- If you want the grout colour to have a high contrast with the tiles, bear in mind that the fixing has to be first class.

It all sounds very fraught, but in reality your chances of having problems are quite small. The situations that give rise to difficulties are really few and far between, but it is better that you know the obvious ones to avoid.

CHAPTER 5

Wall Tiling: Setting Out

GENERAL

Setting out is a vital process in which the tiler usually wanders about for a full day with straight edges, plumb line, long pieces of wood, a level and a pencil behind his ear taking measurements and making marks on the wall. This gives rise to one of the most common complaints made about tilers, "They never fixed a tile on the first day, all they did was measure up." This is quite true, and it is because every tiler knows that if he doesn't get the 'measuring up' right, not only is the tiling not going to look good, but he is going to spend a lot of time putting difficult cuts in awkward places.

Setting out is simply a way of making sure that the tiling is going to look symmetrical and that the best possible compromise (and setting out is all about compromise) is reached regarding the positions of the joints.

It is important for two reasons. The first is that, no matter how well the tiles are fixed, unless the setting out is well done, the job will not look right. The second is that it actually makes the tiling easier to do. Put very simply, the point of setting out is to try to arrange things so that cut tiles are evenly positioned, as large as possible, and that no cut tile is too small or too awkward to do.

An easy way to visualize the setting out process is to imagine a drawing of a wall with a door and a window in it. A piece of tracing paper with the tiles drawn onto it is put on top of your drawing and moved about to see how the tiles fit and what options you have. Placing the tracing paper so that it works whole tiles from the bottom of the window might

Tip

If you don't know where the last tile is going, don't fix the first one.

result in a very narrow cut tile both to the floor and the ceiling. This is both difficult to do and unsightly. Moving the tracing paper down a little will show you that, although you might now have to a cut tile to the window cill, you will have easy and presentable cuts to both the floor and the ceiling. As these cuts have to go around the whole room, you will not only have improved the appearance, you will have made the work of cutting much easier. You will have slightly more cutting to do, but the overall amount of work will be less. We are aiming to keep the cut tiles as large as possible *on average*. There will be situations where narrow, difficult cuts are unavoidable. Keep them to a minimum and try to arrange for these to go in places where they are not obvious. Never put yourself in the position of having to do the impossible.

There is rarely an ideal setting out. To get decent-sized cuts to the sides of a window you may find that you have an awkward and narrow row of cuts to do somewhere else. Personal choice will also play a part in this, as does the design of the tile. You may find that you personally cannot live with unequal cuts on each side of a window, even if it does mean a 10mm cut against the end wall. Because of such preferences there are few golden rules with setting out, but here are a few general ones.

• **Do it thoroughly and accurately**. You may think

51

that it is working out conveniently, with nice whole tiles into the corner to the next wall. But if you have only checked the setting out in one position and that wall is slightly out of plumb you could end up trying to do a very difficult narrow cut.

- **The obvious is not always the thing to do.** Starting with whole tiles from the top of the bath might seem a good idea, but no tiler would ever do it without being certain that everything else in the room worked out.
- **Never make assumptions.** The top of the skirting board is very unlikely to be either level or straight. The bath will probably not be perfectly level either. Window cills will often slope slightly. You want to be working to the levels and lines that you set, not anything that just happens to be there.
- **If you can't avoid it there is no need to make it obvious.** If a room sets out awkwardly and you have a cut that you don't want but cannot avoid, try to arrange for it to go where it won't be noticed – in the corner above the entrance door, for example.
- **The tiler is always right.** There is rarely a perfect setting out and you will have to make compromises. Choose the ones that suit you. You have to live with them.

GETTING STARTED – THE DATUM LINE

Before anything else can be done it is necessary to mark a datum line onto the walls. This is a level and straight line which goes right around the room. As other important measurements are going to be made from it, it is vital that it is both dead level and dead straight. It should be a convenient working height from the floor and ideally be in a position where you can put a continuous line without it being unduly broken up by windows or other openings. It is stressed that a datum line is not intended to mark a tile joint; it is a basis for measurement and nothing else.

Note

In the setting-out drawings, all reference lines such as datum, base and cross lines, that is, lines only intended to be measured *from*, are coloured **red**. Setting out lines, that is, those intended to represent tile joint positions, are coloured blue.

OPPOSITE: A large tile can be used in a small room if the colours are chosen carefully.

RIGHT: The datum line has to be dead level and straight, and is carried right around the room.

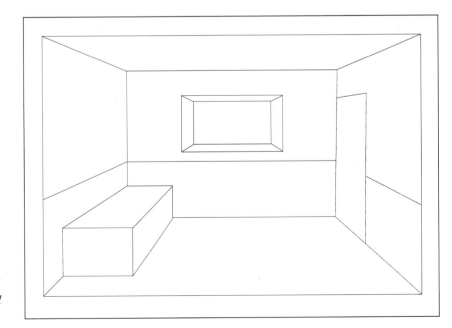

Marking a Datum

Although this can be done single handed it is much easier if you have someone to help with the level and string line.

Using a Spirit Level

Put a horizontal pencil mark on the wall at the height you have decided upon. Take a long spirit level and hold it horizontally against the wall with its left-hand end on the pencil mark. Keep your eyes square onto the bubble and adjust the right-hand end of the level until the bubble is dead centre between the lines. Taking care not to let the level slip, mark the position of the right-hand end of the level. (If you are very confident you can just draw a continuous line using the level as a straight edge.) Reverse the ends of the level. *This is important as it cancels out any inaccuracy in the level and prevents accumulated errors.* Place the left-hand end of the level on the last mark you made. Adjust the right-hand end of the level once more until the bubble is central, then mark the wall at the right-hand end once again. Carry on repeating the process until you arrive back at your starting point. The last mark you make should join up with the first one. With a good level, properly used, the lines will usually be within 1mm to 2mm of each other.

If your pencil lines do not meet, it is usually for one of three reasons:

1. **The level is not accurate**. This is not unusual if the level is old or has been roughly treated.
2. **Inaccurate marking**. This usually causes an accumulative error. It is important that the level is

always positioned exactly onto the last mark and that the pencil point is tight into the corner between the level and the wall when making the next one.
3. **The level has moved**. Silly as it may sound, this is the most common reason. It is remarkably easy for a level to slip without you noticing.

Once the lines do meet, reinforce the datum line using a chalk line. This is simply a piece of fine string covered with coloured powder or coloured chalk dust. With an assistant holding the chalk line firmly onto the pencil mark at one end of a wall, hold it on the pencil line at your end with one hand, pulling the line tight as you do so. Using your free hand, pull the string about 200mm off the wall, as near to the centre as you can reach, and let it twang back to strike the wall. It should leave a clean, clear, dead-straight line, and, if you lined the chalk line up correctly, it will be dead level. Repeat this process on all the walls until the datum line is completed.

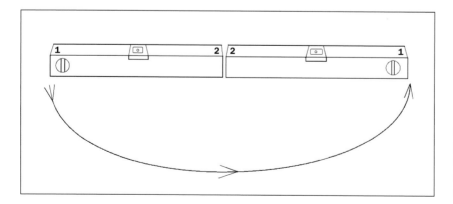

Reversing the ends of a spirit level as you go around the room cancels out any slight inaccuracy in the level.

Striking a datum line.

Using a Laser Level

The setting up of a laser level varies from make to make, and, because of this, it is not possible to give detailed instructions. However, they do all work on the same principle. A rotating platform carrying a laser is set up dead level. Some levels have an internal pendulum which will do this automatically. The beam of the laser will then, in theory, be projected absolutely horizontally and shows as a line or spot of red light on the wall. The laser is then rotated so that the spot moves around the room and its position is marked on the wall until you

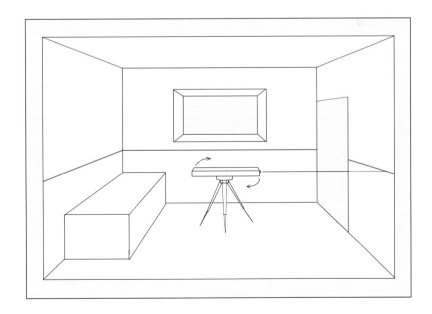

A laser level projects a horizontal beam of light around the room.

*Marking a datum line
with a laser level.*

arrive back where you started. You then join up the dots with a string line as before.

However, you do need to know one thing. *The line generated by a laser level will always meet when you get back to the start, whether it is level or not.* So, once you have marked your datum line, set up the level again with the tripod set at 180 degrees to its original position, line up the laser beam on your pencil marks and rotate the laser again to check them.

THE GAUGE LATHE

You will now need to make the one piece of equipment that you cannot buy – a gauge or gauge lathe. This is simply a long, thin piece of wood with the positions of the tile joints marked on it. Think of it as a large ruler that measures in tiles rather than centimetres.

A section of 50mm × 10mm is about right, but any long thin piece of wood will do providing it is reasonably straight. The length you want will vary with the job, but it needs to be long enough for you to do the setting out, and not so long that it gets in the way. The right length for the average bathroom is about 2m. If in doubt, make a longer one, it is easier to cut one down than to make a new one.

In order to make your gauge you need to know the joint width you are going to use. This should be straightforward, as the tiles will usually be accurate in size. All that is then needed is the use of a standard spacer peg. This will govern the joint width to the thickness of the spacer peg. If there is much size variation in your tiles a slightly different method is used and this is discussed later in Chapter 7.

Lay your piece of wood on a flat surface (usually the floor is the only place long enough). Carefully lay a straight row of tiles flat on the floor with one edge tight up against your lathe. Space the tiles carefully using spacer pegs. Use a peg at both ends of a joint if the tiles won't stay parallel. Push the tiles gently together so that all the joints are even, accurate and the correct width. With your piece of wood against the edge of the tiles, carefully mark the positions of the joint centres with a sharp pencil. Then, as setting out tiles with an inaccurate gauge can give you real problems, lay the tiles out again and check that you have done it accurately.

You will need to use both edges of the gauge. So, using a set square, accurately extend the line right across the width of the lathe. Cut off any surplus wood to the last pencil line at the ends; the end of the wood should be the centre of a joint.

If you are using a rectangular rather than a square tile, you will need to make two gauges, one for the horizontal setting out and one for the vertical.

THE BASIC PRINCIPLES

The setting out of wall tiling is divided into two sections. The first is the horizontal setting out which dictates the position of the horizontal joints. The second is the vertical setting out which does the same thing for the vertical joints.

The horizontal setting is usually the most difficult, as it goes around the whole room and has to take account of the features on all of the walls. The vertical setting out is normally done on a wall to wall basis, as the internal corners are going to break the sequence of tiles anyway.

It is usual to do the horizontal setting out first as it includes striking the datum line for the whole room. It also gets the difficult bit over with.

Horizontal Setting Out

Once the datum has been established the gauge lathe comes into play. If you have two you want the one marked with the horizontal joints. Choose a suitable wall. This is usually the one with the most things that you are going to have to cut to, for example the floor, ceiling, window head and cill, the top of the bath and so on.

Hold the gauge vertically against the wall. You will be able to see how the tile joints are going to relate to all the horizontal places that you are going to have to cut tiles to. Move the gauge up and down until you have arrived at the best average situation. Holding the gauge still, lightly mark the position of the datum line on the gauge.

Move to the next wall and place the gauge vertically against it, with the mark you have just made lined up on the datum. By moving the gauge horizontally whilst keeping the mark aligned with the datum you will be able to see how the setting out you have just done for the first wall relates to the second. If the cutting works out OK, move onto the next wall. If it doesn't and an adjustment is required, raise or lower the gauge as necessary and remark the position of the datum on the gauge. This adjustment will alter the setting out of the first wall. Go back to it, put the new mark on the datum, and see how your first wall has been affected by the adjustment. Repeat the process round the room. Each time you alter your mark you will have to go back over all the previous walls to see that things still work out on them.

You may find that your setting out of the first wall gives totally unacceptable results elsewhere. If it does, it is quicker to go back to the beginning, and raise or lower the gauge to a point that improves the situation. Remark the datum on the gauge and start again.

You will eventually arrive at a situation that is

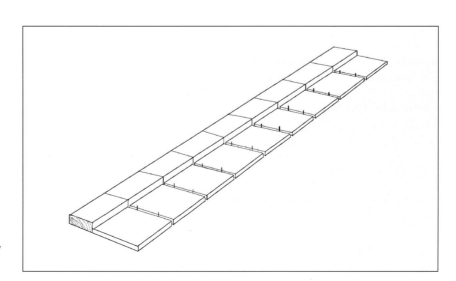

Making a 'gauge' or 'gauge lathe'. The length should be suited to the job.

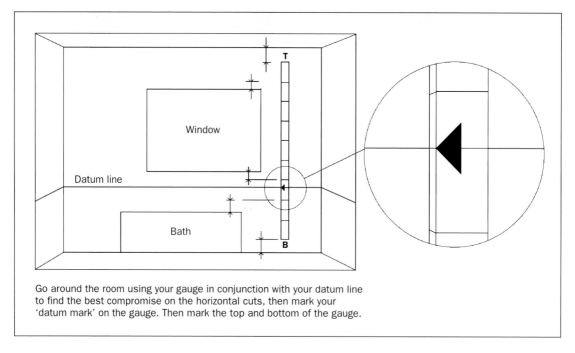

Go around the room using your gauge in conjunction with your datum line to find the best compromise on the horizontal cuts, then mark your 'datum mark' on the gauge. Then mark the top and bottom of the gauge.

Horizontal setting out.

acceptable right around the room. When you do, *the mark indicating the position of the datum on the gauge should be made permanent.* This is your datum mark. When this is lined up with the datum line anywhere in the room, you will be able to see exactly where all the horizontal joints are going to be *Then mark the ends of the gauge 'top' and 'bottom'.* From now on, this gauge can only be used this way up.

In a complicated room you may find that you lose track of all the points you are carrying in your mind – don't worry about it, so do tilers!

Vertical Setting Out

Once the horizontal setting out is finalized we come to the vertical setting out. This is basically the same process as before, but rotated through 90 degrees. It is usually done wall by wall.

Using the gauge (the vertical one this time, if you have two), place it horizontally against the wall and adjust it from side to side until you can see how the tile joints are going to relate to the vertical points that you are going to have to cut up to, for example window reveals, the junctions with adjoining walls

and so on. If the wall is a long one you may need to move the gauge along the wall. This is done by simply marking one of the joint positions on the wall then moving the gauge along until another joint position lines up with it. Because you have only one wall to consider you should be able to assess quite simply how the tiles are going to work out. Try to aim for as symmetrical a setting out as you can. If a wall does set out so that difficult or narrow cuts are unavoidable then the same rules apply as previously. Try to keep them where they are less likely to be seen. This can work to your advantage as there will often be fewer of them to do.

Once you are happy with the setting out, mark one of the vertical joints clearly on the wall in a convenient area to start tiling, ideally a largish area as central to the wall as you can make it. *Using a plumb line strike a full height true vertical line at this point.* This is your vertical setting-out line (VSL) for this wall.

Repeat this process on all the walls of the room.

Because you are doing the vertical setting out one wall at a time there are fewer points to relate to, and

Marking a vertical setting-out line.

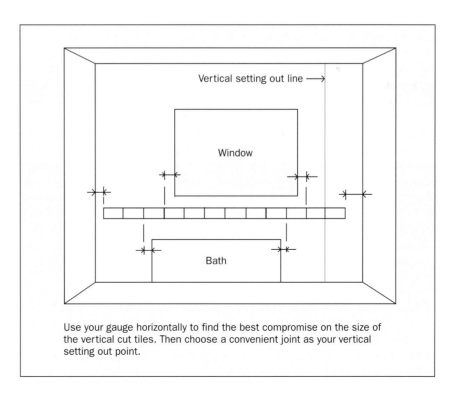

Vertical setting out line ⟶

Window

Bath

Use your gauge horizontally to find the best compromise on the size of the vertical cut tiles. Then choose a convenient joint as your vertical setting out point.

Vertical setting out.

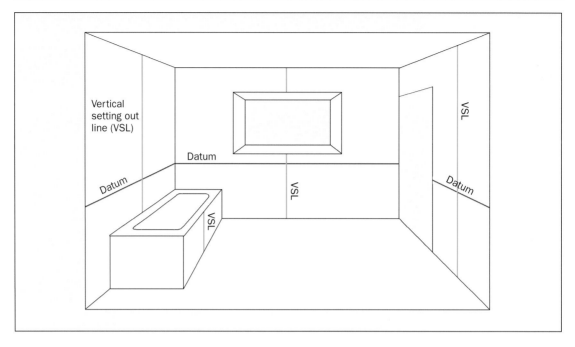

Fully set-out room showing datum line and vertical setting out points.

it will usually be reasonably easy to decide the final joint positions. Just occasionally, it may be necessary to create a true vertical using a plumb line to use as a vertical datum. This will usually only be where the setting out is complicated and/or where the cutting dimensions become very critical. In such a case, the same procedure is used as for the horizontal setting out. The vertical datum is used in combination with the gauge to enable you to relate how the various tile joints will fall.

Always remember that datum lines, either vertical or horizontal, are only there to give you a fixed point to measure from when doing the setting out. They are not part of the tiling grid. Just occasionally, in setting out a room, you will find yourself in a situation where there is no right answer. This is where personal preference comes in and the professional tiler consults with (or passes the buck to, according to your view) his client. In such cases, it is just down to personal preference.

You are now in a situation where you know where all your tile joints will fall and just how big, small or difficult your cut tiles are going to be.

LATHING UP

The next stage is 'lathing up'. This is the fixing of narrow timber lathes to the wall to support and position the tiles as you fix them. The lathes only need to be light – between 40mm and 50mm wide is usual. They should be thick enough to support the tiles properly, but not so thick that they project in front of the tiles as you fix them – 6mm to 8mm is usually about right, depending upon the tile. Try to get straight lathes; they need to be straight once they are fixed and you don't want to have trouble pulling them into line as you fix them.

The intention is to fix all the whole tiles in the first instance, and you will need the lathe both to support them and to ensure they are in the correct horizontal position. Once the adhesive has set the lathes can be removed and the bottom row of cut tiles fixed under them later.

The first lathe should be fixed so that its top is on the line of the first tile joint above the floor. This is your base lathe. Unless you have no alternative, do not be tempted to fix the lathe in a position that will

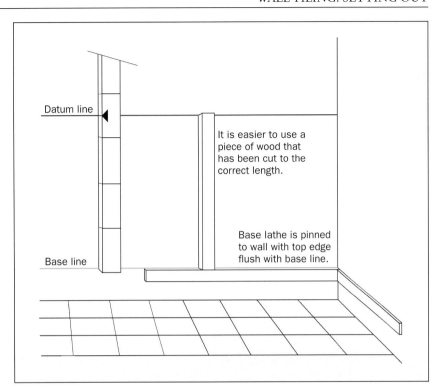

It is easier to use a
piece of wood that
has been cut to the
correct length.

Base lathe is pinned
to wall with top edge
flush with base line.

Datum line

Base line

*Fixing the position of
the base lathe from the
datum line.*

*'Staffing down' from a
datum line to fix the
'base' or bottom lathe.*

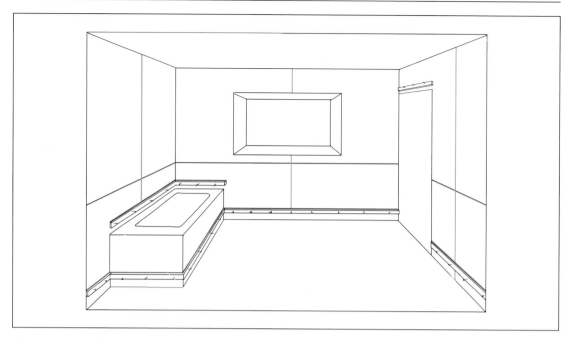

Room set out and lathed up ready for fixing. The lathes above the bath and door should be left off and fixed to the actual tile joint when needed.

leave you more than just the last cut tile to put in at the bottom. It will involve more work.

STAFFING DOWN

Place the datum mark of your gauge on the datum line and mark the position of the appropriate joint onto the wall. Do this around the whole room. This is your baseline. (You may have either to cut or extend the gauge to the correct tile joint.) Pin the lathe to the wall using small nails or hardened steel pins so that its top edge is exactly on the line you have just marked.

A more accurate way to do this is to get someone else to hold the gauge (or a piece of wood cut to the correct length) vertically against the wall with its mark exactly on the datum line. This leaves you free to push your lathe against its bottom end as you pin it. This process is called 'staffing down' and ensures

that the lathe is the correct distance down from the datum, and is parallel to it.

Continue this lathe right around the room. If you are short of lathe there is nothing to stop you reusing the lathe and doing the room wall by wall. If you do reuse lathe make sure it is scraped or wiped clean first. It is amazing how far you can be thrown out by a bit of dry adhesive.

If you are totally confident in your accuracy you can extend your lathes by fitting those over the horizontal positions that you are going to have to cut to, such as the top of a bath, kitchen worktop or a window head. As before, this is done by 'staffing', that is, using your gauge to measure the appropriate number of tiles up the wall and fixing another lathe to carry the first whole tile above the feature. In practice, it is usually better to fit these lathes as and when you need them. You can then fit them to the actual tile joint rather than a theoretical line.

CHAPTER 6

Fixing

Observant readers will probably notice that the tilers in some of the photographs do not appear to be using spacer pegs. They aren't! They are using forty years' experience combined with a commercial non-slip adhesive on a backing they know will not give them trouble. This is not a recommended method for a DIY project. If your tiles start to slide when you have put a few metres on the wall, you will be in for a bad day.

Now you are in a position to start fixing. The lathe will govern the starting position of the horizontal tile joints, and the vertical lines you marked give the vertical ones. You can now start fixing tiles knowing exactly where you are going to finish.

APPLYING ADHESIVE

You now need to apply a coat of adhesive to the wall. The intention is to form even and consistent ridges of adhesive into which the tiles are pressed, the displaced material filling the spaces between the ridges and giving as near continuous a layer of adhesive as possible.

There are two processes involved; the first is the laying on of the adhesive. This means getting a continuous layer in full contact with the wall. The second is the combing off. This is done using the serrated or notched edge of the trowel to form the ridges of adhesive into which you can bed your tiles. To do this involves holding the trowel or spreader blade tight against the wall at as steep an angle as you can comfortably manage. When this is dragged across the wall surface the notches or serrations will leave ridges of adhesive whilst removing the excess. Using a spreader, this is relatively easy. However, it needs a

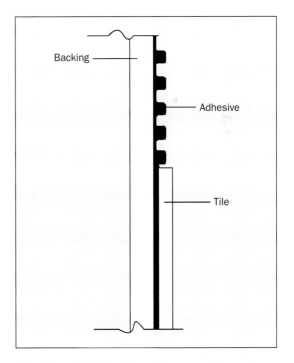

The ridges of adhesive formed by a serrated trowel should squash down to give as continuous a bed as possible.

strong wrist to apply a full notched floating trowel of adhesive and comb it off in one action. Until you get used to it, you may find it easier to do the laying on by making repeated applications with a smaller trowel, using the notched trowel just for combing off.

Try to get nice clean ridges; you may get some lumps of adhesive where you don't want them, such as on top of your lathe, so remove them with a small trowel before you start fixing. Until you get used to it, do not apply too much adhesive at one time or it may skin over before you have time to fix upon it. If it does, your tiles won't stick as well as they should.

If you are tiling a wet area, such as a shower, then the adhesive is used in a different way, known as 'solid bedding'. This is covered in Chapter 7.

Starting at your vertical setting-out point apply a coat of adhesive to the wall for a height of about 600 mm above your lathe for a length you think will be manageable. (If you find you are hiding your vertical setting-out line behind a coat of adhesive, make a mark on your lathe where you can see it.)

PLACING THE TILES

Position the first tile with its bottom edge on the lathe, line up one of its sides with your vertical line and press the tile firmly into the adhesive using a slight twisting movement. Place another tile next to it and repeat the sequence, inserting a spacer peg in the joint between the two tiles whilst pushing them gently together. Make sure the tiles are sitting firmly on the lathe and that they are not leaning in or out. Keep repeating the process until you come to the end of your row in both directions.

Note that spacer pegs are placed end on, as they have to be removed later. Spacer pegs are never left in the joints.

Now check that the top edges of the tiles are flush with each other. Any differences in line or level that are caused by the lathe not being quite straight have to be corrected at this stage. If any tile is low, insert a trowel point between its bottom edge and the lathe, twist gently to lift the tile into the correct position, then slip something into the gap to keep it in place. A spacer peg or a piece of card folded to the right thickness will do; just make sure there is plenty sticking out so that you can remove it later. The idea is to ensure that the top edge of the first row of tiles is dead straight. Once you have done this, you should be able to make real progress.

Repeat the whole fixing process for the second row of tiles, inserting two spacer pegs in the horizontal joint under each tile, about a quarter tile in from each end. Do not be tempted to get away with only using one spacer peg; that is OK for the vertical joints not the horizontal ones. As you go along, try to keep the corners of the tiles flush with their neighbours.

It is vital that you ensure that your tiling is flat and true as you proceed. This is nearly impossible to judge by eye and any deviation will cause trouble later. To do this, place a straight edge horizontally on the face of the tiles to make sure that the surface is flat and the tiles are lineable. Do this both horizontally and vertically. With your straight edge placed

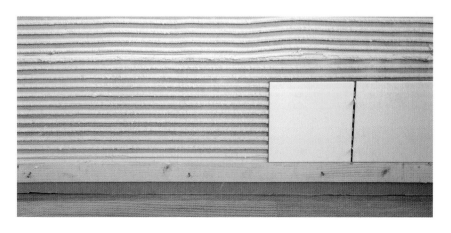

OPPOSITE: Tiles can cater for all tastes.

RIGHT: Try to get the adhesive on the wall as evenly as possible. If the wall is flat it will speed things up considerably.

Fixing the first course of tiles.

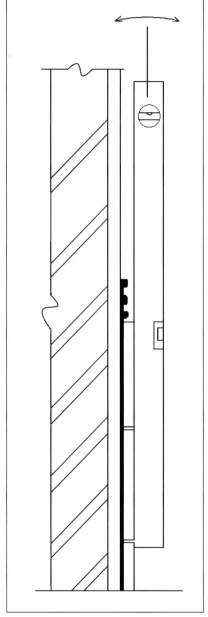

ABOVE: Use a spirit level to make sure that you are not running out of line, either horizontally or vertically.

LEFT: Constantly check your line and level. It is much easier than trying to correct work later.

Here the tiler is 'gridding out' his wall. In this case he has already fixed a contrasting band, which is fixed horizontally. He has to be certain that the joints in the main field, which are to be fixed vertically, will line up.

against the face of the tiling, it should always run parallel to the adjacent backing and should not be leaning either towards or away from the wall. Make sure that all the tile joints are lined up in both directions.

If everything is correct, the process is repeated until all the whole tiles have been fixed for that wall, but it is important that the checking procedures are repeated at regular intervals as you go along.

MAKING ADJUSTMENTS

As tiles sometimes vary slightly in size, occasionally it may be necessary to adjust joints to bring them back into line. The same procedure is used as before – open the joint slightly and insert some packing to keep the tile in its new position. Occasionally you may have to tighten a joint. Just remove the spacer peg and replace it with something a little thinner. I usually just crush it slightly and replace it.

Tip

When opening a joint with a trowel always do it slowly and carefully until you get the hang of it, as too much pressure will damage the tile edge.

This general process of adjusting tiles is sometimes called 'humouring'. Increasing the joint width so that a given number of tiles covers a greater distance is 'gaining'. Decreasing the joint width to cover a lesser distance is (surprise, surprise) 'losing'.

The secret of making adjustments to joints is to do it little and often. You should never need to open or close a joint to a degree that makes it stand out from its neighbours. If corrections have to be made, do them there and then. Once the adhesive has set it will be impossible.

As you proceed, clean up the tiles as much as you can. Any adhesive that has squeezed up into the joints should be removed using a knife blade or the point of a fine trowel and a sponge. Sponge off any adhesive on the tile face. Do it as you go along, as it will be more difficult once the adhesive has set.

MAINTAINING YOUR LINES

When you are tiling around a window or any other obstruction which involves you having to leave out an area of tiles in the middle of a wall it is vital that your vertical setting-out lines are maintained.

For example, you may have a width of fifteen tiles below the window; finding out that you have fifteen and a bit tiles once you are above the window is

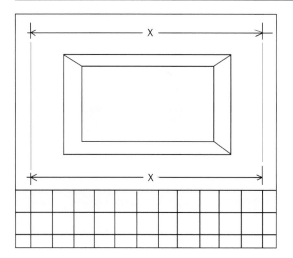

When tiling around windows or other obstructions, extend vertical lines from joints on each side to ensure that you are going to meet accurately.

disconcerting. Even worse, you may find that you do not have the distance to get your fifteen tiles in.

To avoid this situation, once you have a continuous row of tiles below the window, extend a true vertical line from a tile joint on each side of the window to a point above the level of the window head. Check that the measurement between the lines above the window is the same as that between the joints below the window. You can then tile to these lines knowing that you are going to have the same setting out above the window as you did below it and that your tiles will meet properly.

When tiling around openings which have returns to them, such as windows, it cannot be emphasized too much that the tiling should be as flat as possible. Any bow or curve on the face can cause all sorts of problems when you come to tile the returns because you will be trying to follow a curved line with the return tile.

If the walls are flat and you have applied the adhesive evenly, you are not likely to have much difficulty. If a tile is slightly out of line, pressing a tile on one corner or side will cause that one to go in and the opposite one to come out and the tile will line up. At the very worst, you may have to take a tile off and add or remove some adhesive. If you have to do this,

slide the blade of a small trowel or wallpaper scraper behind the tile. With a slight twisting motion, apply gentle but sustained pressure until the suction is broken and the tile comes away. It can then be scraped clean, the back buttered with adhesive and refixed to the correct line.

Once all the whole tiles have been fixed, if there is going to be any delay at all, go around with a scraper and remove any surplus adhesive from the wall outside the area of tiles. Once it has set it will stop you fixing the cuts properly. Tilers will often do this anyway, as cutting can be a slow process and if the adhesive skins over it can prevent the tiles sticking properly. They will then fix the cuts by buttering the backs of the tiles with adhesive.

CUTTING IN

Once all the whole tiles have been fixed we come to the cutting in. The secret of good cutting is accurate marking. Starting at the first tile up from the lathe, carefully measure the width of the space the cut has to go in. From this, deduct a measurement equal to the width of a joint plus an amount for clearance from the wall you are cutting up to. Usually the clearance will be about 3mm or 4 mm, but should never be more than the tile is thick, or you will have a gap you can't cover when you tile the next wall. Transfer the result to a tile and, having cut it, try it in place to see if it fits. If it is too large or needs adjustment trim it with tile nippers. An alternative method is simply to hold the tile in position and mark it directly from the opening, remembering to make allowance for the joint and clearance.

If the tile has a directional pattern you will have to turn it upside down to mark it, as it is the cut edge that is going to go against the wall and the uncut side against the main field. Once you are happy with the fit, smooth off the edge with your abrasive block, butter the back of the tile with adhesive and press it

> **Tip**
>
> Never throw away an incorrectly cut tile. You will often be able to recut it for use somewhere else.

carefully into place until it is both flush and lineable with the main tiling. Place spacer pegs in the joints with the adjoining tiles at both the bottom and the side. Then insert another one, or a piece of folded card, into the joint against the wall. This is to prevent the tile sliding out of position and opening the joint to the next tile. If there is to be any slight irregularity it should be in the joint to the adjacent wall, not the joint in the main field.

If you have a 'raking' or 'splay' cut (one that is out of square), you can 'reverse mark' it. Turn the tile so that the side you are cutting off is towards the main field, not towards the wall. Put the bottom of your tile to the top of the opening you are cutting into, and mark the width you want, allowing for joint and clearance. Then place the top of the tile to the bottom of the opening and do the same again. Join up the two marks and cut on this line. When you turn the tile so that the cut side is against the wall, it should fit exactly (see page 70).

Repeat the process for the next tile up, inserting a spacer peg underneath it to maintain the joint width. A large-sized cut will need one at each end of the joint. The process is then repeated until the whole row of vertical cuts is complete.

It takes practice to be able to cut a tile so that it fits accurately every time. After a while you will find that you will be able to measure a tile and automatically make the allowance for the joints as you cut it. If you have any doubts, cut on the large side. An oversize cut can be trimmed to size, a cut that is too small – is too small.

When cutting to a bath or a shower tray, whether you are using either a silicone rubber sealant or a preformed trim, take particular trouble to get a nice, neat, tight cut. It will help to give a good watertight joint. If you are using a sealant it will also provide a good base and enable you to make a better job of the sealing process later.

The cutting to the ceiling usually presents no

Careful marking of cut tiles is vital …

… if you want them to fit properly.

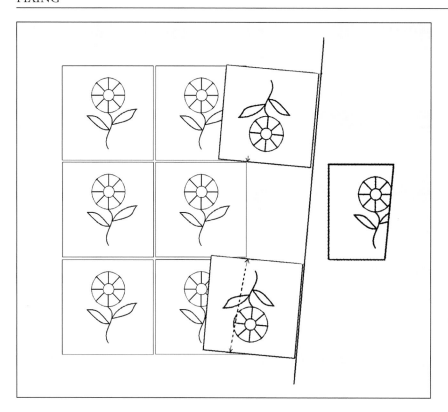

LEFT: *Reverse marking. By inverting your tile you can mark a raking cut directly from the adjoining tiles. When cut and turned around it will be the correct size and angle.*

Tip

For holding perimeter cuts in position a piece of thin, stiff, folded card works better than a spacer peg, particularly when cutting down to an uneven floor. As the folded card tries to unfold it exerts a slight pressure and pushes the tile up against the tiles of the main field. In the 'good old days' before spacer pegs, tile cartons were the universal source of spacers.

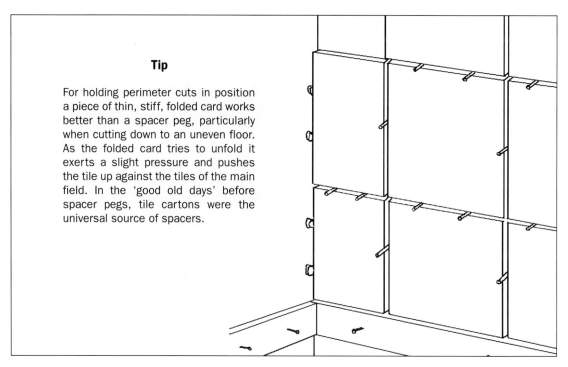

problems, other than it being ladder work. Once the adhesive has set enough to hold the tiles, the last stage is to remove the lathe from under the bottom row of tiles, clean off any blobs of adhesive and then fix the cut tiles down to the floor. Put spacer pegs in the top and side joints as you fix them and hold them in position by wedging with folded pieces of card from the underside. As this will probably involve a lot of lying down, an old cushion can be a real advantage if you don't want sore elbows. Once all the cuts are in, clean up the joints as before.

WINDOWS ETCETERA

Once all the perimeter cuts are in, the next stage is the openings in the tiling that have returns to them, such as windows, and the corners that go with them. A return is the general term used for all those bits of a window or door opening that run back from the face of the wall. Individually they are called cills (or sills, both are correct depending where you come from), reveals and soffits.

Although the side corners should be vertical as they are normally plumbed up, plasterers often judge

> **Tip**
>
> If it is your first tiling job or you think it might be difficult for some reason, set out the whole job but then do a small area from start to finish to get a feel of the processes involved.

> **Tip**
>
> Always check an area *immediately* you finish fixing it. Once the adhesive has set corrections are difficult and a missed spacer peg can mean having to cut a tile out later.

the angle of reveals by eye, and if you measure and cut the face tile to the front corner you may find that you have no choice but to follow the plaster and make your tiling to the returns out of square as well. So check how square and plumb the returns are and whether they need building out. This is particularly important on the soffit, which is the one place where

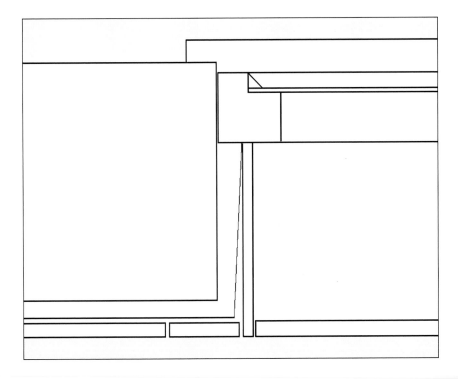

Check window returns so that you can allow enough thickness to square them up.

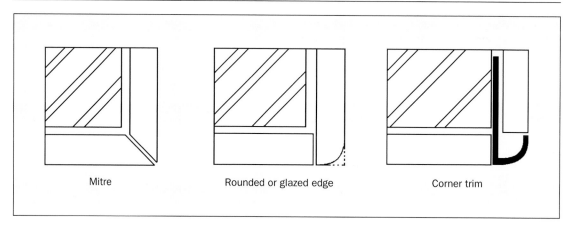

Mitre   Rounded or glazed edge   Corner trim

Alternative methods of forming corners.

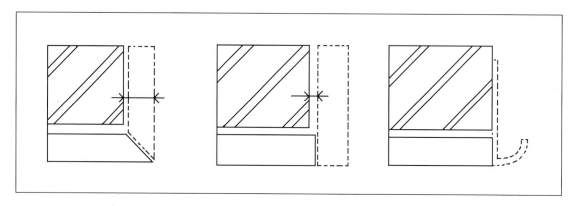

The amount of projection you need to allow over a return will vary with the detail chosen.

you do not want to have any great thickness of adhesive. If they are not too far out you may be happy to leave them as they are, but tiles do tend to show up anything that is out of square more than is the case with paint or wallpaper. If more than a nominal amount of straightening up is needed, make sure that it is fully dry before fixing onto it.

You are now in a position to form the corners and the returns. There are three commonly used methods of forming corners. The most traditional, but becoming much less common, is to butt joint the tiles. This does mean that the tiles that you are using have to be available with either rounded or glazed edges. If this method is used the tiles to the returns always 'master', that is, come over the edge of, the face tile.

An alternative is to mitre the tiles. This method gives a weaker corner, and although it is possible to buy tiles ready mitred, it will mean either mitre cutting some tiles yourself, assuming you have a mitre saw, or having them done for you. A mitre on a cut tile also gives a slightly raw edge and forming mitres to windows can be quite labour intensive. They are occasionally used on decorative work, as it enables the tiles to look as if they are folded around corners like wallpaper. However, it is not a better way of forming a corner, just a different one and it is much more work.

The use of corner trims has largely superseded mitres and is today probably the most common method of forming corners. These are purpose-made plastic or metal extruded sections that are incorporated into the tiling. They give a neat, practical and economical method of going around corners and are easy to use. But be warned, if you smoke, you can permanently damage a plastic trim by putting a cigarette down on it.

The line of the tiles to the returns governs the size of the cuts to the face. Allow only sufficient thickness for the bed if you are butt jointing. Mitred tiles need the tile thickness plus bed thickness. If you are using edge trims you have to allow for the tile plus bed and then deduct from this the thickness of the trim.

Once you have established the size of the cut tiles, the procedure is exactly the same as for any other area. If your setting out is correct and you have maintained your lines, you should be able to do all the cuts to the same size for any particular edge. It is important that, once fixed, the tile edges are straight and lineable, or the joint will look uneven once your returns are fixed.

Let's presume that you are using a plastic corner trim. Start with the reveals. There is no practical reason for this except that the soffit is better left until you have got your hand in, and that it leaves the cill free to put things down on. Fix the notched cut to a bottom corner and the cut tiles above it. Do not skimp on the spacer pegs. Use two to a joint if there is any possibility of the tiles moving. When you get to the notched tile at the top you may need to put a temporary pin in to hold it in position until you can do the soffit. When you have the full row of tiles fixed, cut a length of edge trim a centimetre or so oversize then hold it up to the tiles and mark the length directly from the tiles. Mitre it at both ends. Apply adhesive to the reveal ready to take the tiles. Bed the edge trim in the adhesive, pushing it tight up to the tile edge and making sure that it is flush with the face of the tiled wall. Fix the return tiles from the bottom upwards, making sure that they are flush with the trim and that the joints line up with those on the main wall tiling. If you decide that you are going to cut the bottom tile in last, put a pin, or pins, into the backing to hold your first tile in position.

Check that you are working square to the main wall face. It is very easy to press the tiles further into the bed at the back edge than the front and this can put you out of square and make the bed tight for the next row of tiles. Using corner trims it is easier to fit the return tile before the adhesive of the face cut has set, as its enables you to do any fine adjustments that might be necessary.

This process is repeated on the other reveal and then the soffit; leave the cill to last to give you working space.

The tiles over the top of the window may need to be supported until they have set. Tape them to the tiles above with masking tape after you have put in the spacer pegs.

You should not have any problems sticking the

Tiling a cill. In this case the edge trim was held in position temporarily and the face and return tiles fitted at the same time.

tiles to the soffit unless the adhesive is too thick. However, tiles do tend to move about on soffits, as the adhesive is under tension, so do make sure all the spacer pegs are in position and that they are pushed into the adhesive to stop them dropping out.

Take time to get the mitres to the trims nice and neat and the cutting as accurate as you can. Cills and reveals are areas that tend to get noticed a lot.

If you are using round-edged or glaze-edged tiles and you are confident that your wall is dead straight you can put in all your face cuts before you start on the returns. If you do, let them set and then lightly rub the cut edges with an abrasive block to help give a neat line to fix the returns to. The fitting of the returns is then relatively simple. The joints and line of the face tiling will govern the position of the edge tiles. If the tiling to the wall face is not flat this is where you find out why it had to be, as the return

If corner pieces are not available, the usual method of finishing edge trims at a three-way corner is to mitre the two face pieces and to butt the return piece up behind them. Although fiddly to do, a three-way mitre (shown here) is tidier.

tiles will either 'fan' or 'close up' on you when you try to fix them flush with the face tiles.

The last stage of cutting is the awkward stuff, the cutting around pipes, brackets and so on. Although they are generally done as you come to them, they have to be the last tiles fixed in an area. This is because the relationship with the adjoining tiles has to be known exactly if they are to be marked accurately.

CLEANING UP

Once all the tiles have been fixed the next process is the cleaning up. Ideally you will have done as much of this as you could as you went along. Leaving all the cleaning down to the end can give problems, as some adhesives can be difficult to remove if they are left for too long. The best time is when the adhesive has set enough to hold the tiles, but before it has fully hardened. Epoxy and similar materials can be impossible to remove once they have set and so these *must* be properly cleaned off as you use them.

Cleaning down after fixing.

Grouting up.

Assuming that the adhesive has set and there is no chance of the tiles slipping, the first stage is to remove all the spacer pegs. Most will come out with your fingers, but there are always some that will have stuck to the adhesive. It is usually easier to go around pulling them out with a small pair of pliers.

The walls should be washed down with a damp sponge to remove any traces of adhesive from the tiles. Adhesive showing in the joints should be removed with a knife or trowel point, taking care not to damage the tiles. Any stubborn traces on the tile face are better removed by using a piece of wood as a scraper, as steel tools will occasionally mark tiles. The tiles should be clean and there should be nothing in the joints that would show once the tiles have been grouted.

Tip

When cleaning out your grout or adhesive bucket be careful how you dispose of the slurry. Grout and cement-based adhesives set rock hard and can block your waste pipe and/or drains.

GROUTING

Once all the tiles are nice and clean the next process is the grouting. Traditionally this used to be the apprentice's job, supervised by the tiler. It freed the tiler to get on with other things and by the time the apprentice had finished his apprenticeship it had become a conditioned reflex. He would find it difficult to do a bad grouting job if he wanted to.

The first thing you will find out about grouting is that it is messy, so cover everything up that you don't want to have to clean later. The second is that it can be very hard on the hands, so wear gloves. The third thing is that no one seems to know how thick grout should be. If the instructions give a measured quantity of water that is fine, but they usually say something like 'mix with clean water to a creamy consistency'. This gives you the option of mixing it anywhere between very runny indeed and clotted cream.

The point to remember is that we want to fill the joint. Mix the grout too thick and it will not fill the joint properly, too thin and it will be unworkable. It

Tooling or 'pegging off' a joint.

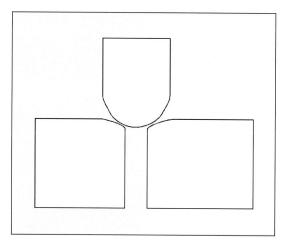

A piece of wooden dowel with a carefully rounded end is used to 'tool back' the grout to a consistent line.

should be quite sloppy to the extent that it is difficult to handle with a trowel, but stiff enough to cling to the tiles without running down the face too much. The only time that you will need to mix grout thicker is if you are using a tile that needs wide joints, when it has to be thick enough to stay in the wider joint. Grout stiffens up as you use it, and if in doubt you are better a little on the thin side.

Work in an orderly manner from the top down to avoid having to clean grout off areas that you have already done. Keeping the bucket as close to the wall as you can, take some grout on a soft-faced floating trowel or squeegee and quickly spread it onto the face of the tile. Try to do it in one movement. There is a knack to doing this, as the moment you lift your squeegee out of the bucket the grout is going to want to run onto the floor. The secret is to get it spread on the tiles before it has the chance. Little and often is best until you have the hang of it. Once you have

---

> ### Tip
>
> When grouting and/or sealing down to the top edge of a bath, do it with the bath full of water. Baths take a lot of weight in use and often settle slightly and open up the joint, particularly when new.

sufficient grout on the wall work it into the joints using the squeegee in a figure of eight pattern until all the joints are full. Sometimes air bubbles will get trapped in the joints and then burst, leaving little bits of unfilled joint, so check your work as you go along. Once you are happy that the joints are properly filled, go over the area again to clean off all the surplus grout that you can. At this stage the joints should be slightly overfull.

TOOLING OFF

As the grout sets, it reaches a point where it is no longer liquid and crumbles readily when scraped. This is the point at which you need to 'peg off' or 'tool off' the joints. Do not use a metal tool for this as it can create marks. This is best done with a piece of wood which you have rounded slightly at one end. (This is sometimes called a 'peg' from the resemblance to the old wooden clothes pegs.) The size will vary with the joint width. The idea is to cut the grout back to a neat, even line on the edge of the tile. Simply run the rounded end of the wood along the joint and the surplus grout will flake off. If it doesn't, the grout is still too wet. The secret is to catch it just at the right time, after the initial set has taken place but before the grout has fully hardened. You will soon learn when to do this, as correct timing makes the job easy to do. It is important that you do not leave this process for too long as it will become more difficult as the grout sets.

Go over all the joints in a systematic manner to make sure that you don't miss any. You will find that you will expose some places where the grout hasn't penetrated. Fill these with a little grout, the tip of a gloved finger is best for this, then run the 'peg' over it again.

CLEANING DOWN

Once you are happy that the joints are even and smooth go over the tiles with a damp sponge to remove all the surplus grout. Do this thoroughly, but do it lightly without any great pressure. It is important that you do not use too much water in this

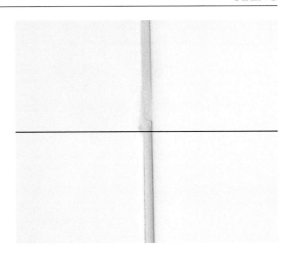

The effect of 'pegging off'. Below the line has been done, above the line hasn't. You can see the difference.

Cleaning down after grouting. The tiler here is using a professional sponge-faced floating trowel.

Polishing off.

process and that you do not try to get the tiles completely clean. As you remove the surplus grout you will find that the tiles are left with a light scum of grout on the face. If you try to remove this you will pull grout from the joints onto the face of the tile. This will spoil the line of the joints and your tiling still will not be clean. Once you have got to the 'clean but scummy' stage, leave it and get on with something else until the grout has fully hardened, usually the following day.

POLISHING OFF

Once the grout is fully set it is not affected by water and you can clean away to your heart's content without any risk of spoiling the joints. It is usually easier to go over the tiling with a dry cloth first. A wet cloth tends to move the scum around, rather than remove it. This can be a dusty job so close the door and wear a light dust mask if you do it this way. Finally, wipe over with clean water to remove the dust, using a sponge or cloth.

CHAPTER 7

Wall Tiling Variations

This section deals with those bits which you might need to know, but that are outside the scope of the basic tiling process.

SOLID BEDDING

'Solid bedding' is a fixing technique which is used in wet areas or anywhere that a high strength bond is needed.

The idea is to get the bed as solid as possible so that there are no voids behind the tiles. It is used where the tiles are going to be vulnerable for some reason. In wet areas there is always some danger of water penetrating the joints and if it remains there it can cause damage to either the adhesive or the backing. In such cases the idea is to give the water nowhere to go. Properly done, the basic serrated or notched trowel method of fixing gives a good coverage but is rarely total. In solid bedding a special trowel can be used which gives a very even, dense coverage. Additionally, the whole back of the tile can be carefully covered in adhesive before it is applied to the wall.

In wet areas, such as showers, it is better to put a layer of adhesive on both surfaces and then to check the top edge of each course of tiles to make sure that there are no voids behind the tiles. If there are, 'back fill' them with a pointing trowel as you go along.

With 'solid bedding' there should be no voids behind the tiles.

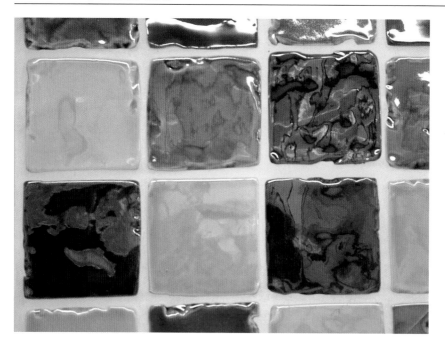

LEFT: With irregular tiles the joints will vary in width as the tiles vary in size. The joint width has to be large enough to allow for this.

OPPOSITE: High-contrast colour schemes can be very effective.

HANDLING SIZE VARIATION

Sometimes, particularly if you are using handmade tiles, you will find that the tiles vary in size to an extent that makes it difficult or impossible to fix them using standard spacer pegs. This will mean increasing your joint size to take up the size variation and then fixing the tiles by eye. If the manufacturer recommends a joint size then that is fine; if not, you will need to find out how much variation you have.

Select about ten to fifteen tiles at random and stand them together on edge like a pack of cards. You will soon see if there is any size variation. If there is, take out the largest and smallest of the tiles and set them aside. Do this at random from the whole of your consignment. The more times you do it the more accurate the result will be. Usually five or six times will suffice. The tiles you have set aside will be representative of the largest and smallest tiles in the batch. Use these to make your gauge lathe. Lay the

tiles out as before, but instead of using spacer pegs set the joints by eye. The joints will vary in width as the tiles vary in size. Adjust the joint width until you are happy that the joints are at such a width that the size variation in the tiles isn't too obvious. The idea is that the joints are increased in size to a point where they can take up the size variation in the tiles without it showing. Then mark your gauge lathe as before, but this time show both sides of the joint, not just the joint centre.

When it comes to fixing them, such tiles have to be fixed by eye and it is difficult to use spacer pegs as the joints are not going to be constant in width. A 'high grab' or 'non-slip' adhesive is best. Unless they are very heavy, the tiles will stay where they are put when fixed in these materials. You will have to keep checking the tiles with your gauge as the spacing will not be automatic and you easily 'gain' or 'lose' by accident on your setting out, that is, a set number of tiles covering a larger or smaller distance than you intended.

'Quarry' tiles. One of the most basic and traditional of all floor tiles, and one of the toughest.

CHAPTER 8

Floor Tiling

With floors it is vital that you get everything right. Floor tiling installations are stressed in ways that wall tiles never are and, if the tiling is not done properly, it will show very quickly. Floors have to be tough because, to state the obvious, people are going to walk all over them. The tiles also have to be hard enough, and tough enough, to stand up to the *worst* that you are going to give them, not just the average wear and tear of everyday life. Floors get heavy tables trundled across them and cast-iron casseroles dropped on them. They even get damaged by the vagaries of fashion. In the 1960s, when stiletto heels on ladies shoes were all the rage, a huge amount of damage was done to tiled floors and many expensive hardwood, and even marble, floors, were ruined. Whatever you lay, make sure it can stand up to the worst traffic that it is going to get.

The tiling of floors is one area where the quality of fixing really counts. A small area of hollowness behind a wall tile is usually not that important and will probably go unnoticed for the life of the tiling. On a floor the chances are that a chair leg will find it in the first week, and crack the tile.

Tiles are not usually strong enough to stand up to traffic by themselves. They need to adopt the strength of a good, sound subfloor. The idea is that we are trying to apply a hard-wearing, decorative, but not necessarily very strong, finish to something that is strong enough to provide what the tile cannot. The subfloor provides the strength, the tile provides the wearing surface.

Properly done, a ceramic tile floor can last a very long time indeed and will usually outlast the tiler, fashion and, on occasion, the building it is in. We have all walked on floors hundreds, and sometimes thousands, of years old. If you are going to construct something that can last that long you may as well put the effort in.

In the modern domestic situation, adhesive fixing is by far the most popular method and for good reasons. There is rarely enough thickness allowed in modern housing for sand and cement fixing and the use of adhesive enables the floor to be laid more quickly and with less mess. Because of this, and the fact that the basic techniques are the same anyway, the main descriptions here are on the basis that this method of fixing is going to be used.

However, because ceramic tile and marble floors were traditionally laid in sand and cement, and in commercial work often still are, this method is covered in a separate section.

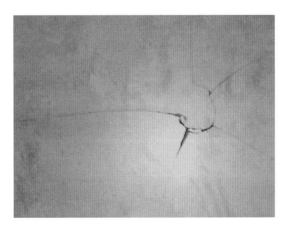

Pressure damage to a floor tile that has not been solidly bedded.

GETTING THE JOB READY

The same rules apply here as for wall tiling. Make sure that the floor is clear and that everything that has to be removed is out of the room before you start work. You do not want to have to carry anything heavy across your newly laid floor just because you couldn't be bothered to move it before you started. When you start work you need to be able to get at the whole floor, so that you know what conditions apply over the total area, not just part of it. All work that needs to be done by other trades, such as the plumber's first fixing, should be complete so that you can cut neatly around pipes and so on. You do not want to have to cut holes through a newly laid floor to get a pipe or a wire through. Apart from being harder work than doing it before you tile, it can result in loose tiles. Newly laid tiles do not like being disturbed.

Ideally, timber skirting should be removed for refixing afterwards; it always looks neater and also means that your cutting does not have to be so precise.

Lighting

As with wall tiling, floor tiling should be done under lighting conditions as close as possible to those which will apply when the floor is in use. If this is not possible then bear in mind how much a narrow light angle can affect the appearance of a floor. A room which has a window that comes right down to the floor should be tiled by daylight. Work away from the light, so that you can see any shadows thrown by the tiles lipping and make corrections as you go along. In such a situation, a floor laid by artificial light shining square onto the face of your tiles can look like a badly laid council pavement the next morning, even if it has been well laid.

Any tiled floor, even if well laid, can look terrible if the lighting conditions change.

Movement and Movement Joint

No one wants these on floors but unfortunately they are sometimes necessary. Movement never really stops on buildings. They move as the materials in them expand and contract with temperature and moisture. Some movement only occurs once, but can take years to occur, such as when a concrete floor slab dries out. You can end up in situations where the floor slab has shrunk as it dried out whilst the tiles expand when the room warms up. If the tiles are getting bigger and the thing they are stuck to is getting smaller, eventually something has to give. Due to their relative strengths, it is usually the tiles. (Movement due to the tile and the base having different movement characteristics is called 'differential' movement.)

You can also get stress from 'deflection'. This is simply the bending of the floor that happens when you trundle your grand piano out into the middle of a room. As the floor sinks in the middle the edges of the tiles get squashed together and can either splinter or come loose. Movement joints are there to prevent, as far as possible, movement of the building damaging the tiling.

There are two main types, which serve different functions. The first are the 'structural' joints that are placed over points in the subfloor which are expected to move. The others are the 'differential movement' or 'stress-relieving' joints which are there to split the tiling down into panels. The idea is that any individual panel should not be big enough for the stress to build up sufficiently to cause problems. There is also a third type, constructed in the same manner as a stress-relieving joint, which is intended to accommodate deflection.

In domestic work the need for movement joints is usually very limited, but as I do not know if your floor is 3m or 30m long it is as well for you to know about them.

BASES

The base is to a floor what a backing is to a wall. It is the thing to which you fasten your tiles. The quality of the base is everything. Just as in wall tiling, the tiling will be as good as the thing to which it is stuck, and it pays to take the time and trouble to get it right.

Tip

If you have any doubts at all about how much floor clearance you have on any door that opens into the room you are going to tile, take the door off. Once you have tiled, if you can't open the door properly you may not be able to get at the hinges to do it. If it is the only door into the room it could take you years to live it down!

The requirements for a base are pretty much those that you would want for any tiling. It has to be strong enough to do the job, straight enough to allow you to tile it, and stable enough not to cause problems later.

Types and Suitability

The best base for hard tiling of any type is undoubtedly concrete. It is very strong and stable and it is possible to stick tiles to it very well. The concrete may have a 'tamped' or 'rough' finish. This is the standard lumpy and bumpy finish left on the floor by the 'tamp', the long, heavy straight edge used to level and consolidate the concrete. Such floors are normally intended to receive a levelling screed of sand and cement. It may have already been screeded ready to receive a finish, or the concrete itself may have been 'trowelled up' (made smooth) ready to receive a floor finish.

If the floor has a tamped finish it will usually need to be screeded. A screed is simply a layer of material that is laid to an uneven floor to level it up. A heavily tamped floor will need to be screeded in sand and cement, usually between 40mm to 50mm thick, to provide a flat, level surface. If this is the case, the builder will have, or should have, left the floor 'down' to receive the screed. This means leaving enough thickness for the screed to be laid.

If a very fine tamp has been used, or the floor has not been finished well enough to allow you to lay the tiles directly onto it, it may be possible to level the floor up using a proprietary levelling compound. These are adhesive-like compounds that are mixed with water and spread over the floor to fill up hollows and provide a level surface to fix to. Whatever finish is on the floor when you take it over, before you start tiling it has to be flat, true, clean and

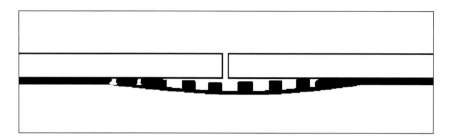

A hollow in the base can result in a floor tile being unsupported at a critical point.

free from dust. Ideally, it should not be smooth in the sense of being smooth to the touch, but should have what is known as a 'wood float' finish. This is the finish left when the screed or concrete is trowelled up with a wooden (nowadays usually plastic) floating trowel. It should have the texture of a coarse sandpaper.

In older houses timber floorboards are one of the most common flooring materials. On newer properties it is 'particle' board (chipboard or similar).

Timber in any form is not as stable as concrete. This is because it constantly moves with atmospheric moisture and is more liable to 'deflect under load', that is, bend when subjected to weight. It is perfectly possible to produce a good, sound floor on a timber base. It just needs careful preparation.

A point that needs mentioning here is that there is a 'trade-off' between the strength of the subfloor and the strength of the tile. If you are laying onto a concrete subfloor the tiles only have to provide a wearing surface. The concrete provides the structural strength. However, with timber subfloors the strength of the tile can play a bigger part.

For example, if you were laying 225mm × 225mm × 30mm (9in × 9in × 1¼in) industrial quarry tile onto a timber subfloor in your bathroom, the strength of this tile is such that, providing the subfloor holds the tile up and the adhesive holds the tile down, there is not a lot that is going to happen to the tiles. They will be strong enough to stand any stress put onto them by movement in the subfloor and, at the worst, you would probably just get some loose tiles, as the bed would probably give way before the tile did.

However, there are not many tiles as strong as a 225mm × 225mm quarry tile and you are not likely to be using those in your bathroom. If you are using

a thinner and weaker tile and the subfloor moves, then the tile might crack long before the adhesive gives way.

From this, you will be able to see that, within limits, a stronger tile does give you a better chance of avoiding problems with the subfloor, or at least makes such problems more manageable. Unfortunately, there is no formula that I can give you for this. The stronger a tile is, the less likely it is to be damaged by movement of the subfloor. It is purely a matter of judgment. If the tile is not a particularly strong one then take every precaution that you can and do your preparation properly.

Existing floors can sometimes be overlaid with hard floor tiles providing they are of a suitable type. Existing ceramic or marble tiles, terrazzo, granolithic and similar materials are all suitable for overlaying. However, the same rules apply to them as for any other base. They must be solid, sound, free from defects and, as existing floors may have been polished or sealed, thoroughly clean. You want the tiles to stick to the floor, not to anything that happens to be on top of it.

PREPARATION

The proper preparation of the subfloor is important for two reasons. The first is that it is important to have a sound and solid base to which to stick, as your tiles are going to depend upon it. The second is that if your base is not reasonably flat it is going to make fixing difficult and can result in your tiles being 'hollow' (that is, not solidly bedded).

If your subfloor is concrete and has been screeded check it by tapping with a light hammer or other hard object to check that the screed is well stuck down. Any parts that aren't will sound 'hollow'; it is quite a distinctive sound and you are not likely to miss it. A tiny bit may not be that important, but generally hollow areas should be cut out and replaced. Check that the floor is clean, flat and level and that there are no loose 'over-runs'. These are the thin layers of concrete that sometimes get smeared across the face of one area of concrete when the next one is laid. If there are any, chop them off – you don't want to fix to anything that may come loose later.

Timber subfloors, because the movement characteristics are so different from those of most floor tiles, often need extensive preparation. It is very important that the floor is made as rigid and stiff as possible. If there is any serious amount of 'bounce' on a timber floor then it may even be necessary to take up the boarding and to stiffen the floor joists with timber noggins.

The British Standard for floor tiling calls for all timber floors, even ones especially constructed to take ceramic tiles, to be overlaid with plywood, in addition to the usual boarding. In the case of existing timber floors it recommends that these should be overlaid with minimum 15mm plywood and that this should be sealed on the underside and edges to prevent it absorbing atmospheric moisture. This is

then screwed down at not greater than 300mm centres to both the underlying boards and, where possible, through into the joists.

There are good reasons for this. One is that joints in the floorboards are often free to move and deflect where they run transverse to the joists. The plywood bridges these and prevents the movement being transferred to the tiles. Another is that 'bounce' or 'spring', that is, the tendency for a timber floor to move up and down when you jump on it, is undesirable in a floor to which you are going to stick tiles. When the overlaying is done properly, and particularly where there are sufficient fixings into the joists, it has the effect of laminating the floor and stiffening the whole construction up considerably.

It will not always be possible to stick to the principles required by the British Standard, but the closer you can get to them the better. In any event, 12mm exterior grade plywood should be considered the minimum and this should be sealed with a non-water-based sealant on the underside and edges before it is fixed. I personally prefer to see the screws at a minimum of 225mm centres rather than 300mm. The joints in your plywood overlay should *never* coincide with those below them in the

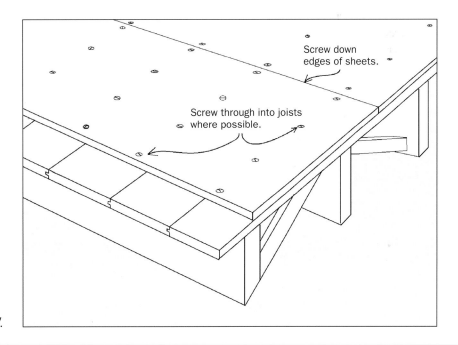

Screw down
edges of sheets.

Screw through into joists
where possible.

*Overlaying a timber
sub-floor with plywood.*

floorboarding. If you can arrange for the length of your sheets to run at right angles to the floorboards or panels below them, so much the better. When problems do occur with a timber subfloor they often occur over the joints in the plywood overlay, as this is the only place where movement can show itself, so you should pay particular attention to screwing the sheets down where their edges meet. The more precautions you take, the less chance you will have of problems later.

A refinement on this, which is sometimes possible on a small floor, is to set out the floor before you fix the overlay, and arrange for the plywood sheet joint to be directly under a tile joint. Then if there is any movement it will open up a joint rather than crack tiles and will be much easier to repair.

Plywood should be stored in the place where it is going to be fixed (or in a similar environment if this is not possible) for a couple of weeks or so to equalize its moisture content before it is fixed. You want any moisture movement to happen *before* the plywood is fixed, not afterwards. The longer you can give it the better.

One word of warning, be particular when buying your plywood. The BS recommends a WBP (Water and Boil Proof) exterior plywood. Other types will do the job in many situations, but some types, such as the shuttering grades of plywood (i.e. plywood intended as formwork for concrete), are simply not intended for this type of use. Some boards are also fireproofed and this can have a serious effect on the ability of adhesives to stick to them, so check if you have any doubts.

As with wall tiling, there are now proprietary boarding systems that can be used for overlaying floors. A further development has been the introduction of 'uncoupling' matting. This is polyethylene matting that is used as an underlay to the tiles. The matting is composed of two layers and is designed so as to permit some movement between them. The principle is that the bottom layer is stuck to the base and the tiles are then stuck to the top layer of the matting. The idea is to prevent any problems with the base affecting the tiling. As it is also waterproof it can be used in conjunction with the sheet material mentioned in the wall tiling section so as to protect the structure from water damage. As with all proprietary systems, the manufacturer's instructions and usage recommendations should always be followed.

Is the Floor Flat Enough? – Correcting Deviations

There will be much more about this in the setting-out section, but a floor should be flat enough to enable you to fix the tiles within the limits of use described by the adhesive manufacturer. Generally, this will mean that a 2m straight edge placed on the surface of the subfloor should not have a gap under it of more than 5mm or so.

If there are places where there is enough undulation to give you problems when you come to fix your tiles they are better dealt with before you start fixing the tiles. Trying to thicken your bed over low areas of floor can give all sorts of problems.

To correct a floor you can either cut off the high

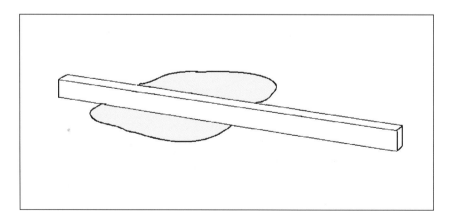

Fill any slight hollows with cement based adhesive or levelling screed and rule off with a straight edge. Leave to dry thoroughly before tiling.

spots, fill in the low spots or do both to arrive at an average. On a concrete floor any odd high spots can be cut off. If only a small area of hollowness is involved and it isn't too deep then a skim with adhesive ruled off with a straight edge a day or two before you start fixing will usually do the job, but allow it to dry thoroughly.

Anything more than this and you are better off using a levelling compound. These are purpose-made materials intended only for levelling up floors. Many have the advantage that they are 'self-levelling' – that is, they are very runny when mixed and find their own level as you spread them. You cannot do this with wooden floors, as levelling compounds are not (usually) suitable for use on timber. If your floor is timber and you know that you are going to have problems with the level, then consider levelling up the floor before you fix the plywood overlay.

CHOOSING A TILE

Location

Where a tile is going to be used usually dictates, at least in part, the type and form of tile chosen. Tiles intended for a room that sees occasional use and which will always have a rug or carpet on top are not going to need to be as tough as those used in an entrance hall or a utility room. In a shower room where there is going to be water on the floor, non-slip properties are important. For an external patio, frost-resistance is essential. Suit the tile to the area.

Usage

The use that tiles will get can sometimes be surprising. I have often been asked "How long will this floor last?" I usually reply "Do you mean the bit in the doorway or the bit under the dresser?" to make the point that the same floor can get hugely differing amounts of wear in different areas. Normally a sun lounge would see quite light usage, but not if part of the floor is also the main route in and out of the kitchen. So consider the amount of wear the floor is going to get in the worst situation. Glazed floor tiles are usually graded for their ability to stand up to abrasion and, if you look hard enough, there is usually quite a bit of other information available as well.

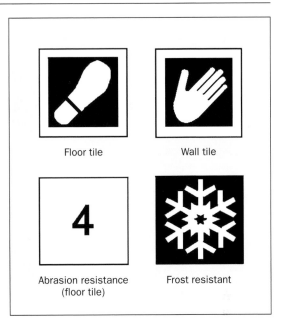

European and British Standard recommended symbols for tile packaging and literature.

Information which is usually somewhere, either on the tile cartons or the manufacturer's literature, includes:

- Maker's name or mark.
- Quality grade – (1st or 2nd etc.).
- European or British Standard reference.
- Tile size – both nominal and working, and whether or not the tile is modular.
- Surface (glazed or unglazed).
- The slip resistance of the tile.
- For glazed tiles – the abrasion class; from grade 0 to grade 5 (grade 0 is no good for flooring and grade 5 is the toughest).

You may also find little pictures on the boxes. A picture of a tile with a footprint on it means that they are floor tiles. If it is a glazed floor tile a number from 0 to 5 gives the class of abrasion resistance. A tile with a hand on it means a wall tile and a tile with a snowflake symbol on it means that the tile is frost-resistant.

Where there is very hard usage and particularly where there is a likelihood of impact on a floor surface, such as in a garage, then unglazed tiles

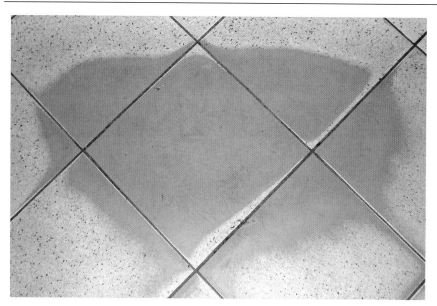

The tile body can show if the glaze wears through.

should be considered. This is because, no matter how tough a glaze is, it is always going to be thin enough to wear through eventually, or be damaged by impact. Once you are through the glaze the colour of the tile body will show through. With an unglazed tile the whole thickness is the wearing surface and you are very unlikely to wear them out. The heaviest commercial 'quarry' tiles and some modern porcelain tiles can stand practically anything you can throw at them.

A bit of technical stuff now. All ceramic materials have a property of density and hardness which, in tiles, is usually referred to as the 'vitrification'. It is quite a complicated subject technically, and this is a simplification, but for our purposes it is enough to know that the higher the degree of vitrification, the harder, and denser, the tile is likely to be. The degree of vitrification is usually measured by working out how much empty space there is within the body of the tile and this is done by seeing how much water the tile will absorb. At the top of the scale are the porcelain and 'fully vitrified' floor tiles, which will absorb practically nothing and are incredibly hard. At the bottom is terracotta, which can be very absorbent and soft. Between these extremes is the general run of floor tiles, both glazed and unglazed.

Absorbency matters because, if a tile will absorb more than about 3 per cent of its volume, there is a

danger of the tiles being damaged by frost. So check that the tiles you want to use on your patio are suitable. (They will usually have been tested and certified by the manufacturer.)

Terracotta – A Special Case

If you are thinking of using terracotta, and I mean genuine terracotta not the modern imitations, then you need to be aware of its properties and the slightly different techniques that are needed, both for laying and maintenance. The term 'terracotta' (Italian for baked earth) is not a specific type of tile, but was, and still is, a general term for a huge range of cheap, unglazed earthenware materials used throughout the Mediterranean region. Fired at a low temperature they are usually, but not always, red in colour with an attractive variegated appearance. They are also soft and absorbent, easily stained and, because of the method of manufacture, often irregular in size and distorted in shape.

It is these features that have made this particular material desirable. People admire the old floors in the 200-year-old villa they rent in Tuscany and want the same antique look in their kitchen at home. The problem is usually that the original floor has had 200 years in which to develop its patina. Originally, terracotta tiles were a cheap way for a rural community to put a cleanable surface onto a floor. They can, in the form in which they were originally laid, look distinctly tatty early in their life when they are starting to stain from the ravages of everyday life. A hundred years of sweeping and washing does, however, build up a nice finish.

Today, people want their floors to look good from day one and this is achieved by sealing and/or waxing the tiles to give the effect of 200 years of wear, tear and loving care.

Terracotta floors can look beautiful, but accept the material for what it is and be prepared for more maintenance than with most modern ceramics.

Size

Although the size of the tile may not seem that important it can occasionally make all the difference in your ability to do a good or bad job. The size of a tile has an effect on what you can do with it. If the subfloor is dead flat, a large tile is quicker to lay, cut and grout than a small one. If the subfloor is not dead flat, it is also going to be more difficult to bed solidly.

If you have problems with the levels and you are going to have to 'twist' the floor in (see Chapter 9), then a big tile can make it impossible to do the job well, as lips will be inevitable.

Tip

Never assume that a floor will be waterproofed by tiling it, no matter how the tiles are fixed. Any waterproofing has to be done in the structure *before* you tile. The best a tile can do is to give the floor some resistance. You may be lucky but don't count on it.

CHOOSING A FIXING METHOD

Adhesives

You generally have less choice of fixing methods with floors than you do with walls. This is because wall tile adhesives only have to do one job – hold the tile onto the backing. A floor tile adhesive has to do two. It has to hold the tile down, but it has also to hold it up. Whatever you use to bed a floor tile with is going to have to stand a lot of pressure. The whole point of a flooring adhesive is that, apart from sticking the tiles down, it has to be hard enough and strong enough to transfer any pressure down onto the subfloor. If it isn't, the tile will break or become loose.

For this reason the majority of floors are laid in

Terracotta isn't always red.

cement-based adhesives. These set by chemical reaction rather than just by drying out, as is the case with many wall tile adhesives. They are also much stronger and tougher and are unaffected by water once they have set. They come in various forms, depending upon the manufacturer. There are the basic adhesives which are simply mixed with water. These are fine on concrete or sand and cement screeded floors, but on timber you will need a modified version.

These have a resin added which gives the adhesive some flexibility and also gives it more 'grab' (makes it stickier). Depending on the manufacturer and type chosen, the modifying resin may be added at the mixing stage as a liquid, or it may be already incorporated in the dry material. A primer may be necessary depending upon the material and the usage. White, as well as the usual grey, is available and this is important if you are fixing translucent, or marble, tiles. These adhesives also come in rapid-hardening versions, which are handy if you need to walk on the floor soon after laying. Be careful with these though, as they are not usually suitable for wet situations.

There are also 'thick bed' types of adhesive. These enable you to lay the floor thicker than with the standard adhesive. Don't take these too much for granted, however, and follow the maker's instructions carefully, as there is a limit to what you can do with them.

There are also synthetic-reaction resin tile adhesives, usually epoxy-based, which can be used for floors. These are very much special case materials and are unlikely to be needed in a domestic situation. They are also usually much more expensive.

Sand and Cement

With the exception of a few specialized applications, sand and cement fixing is the only real alternative to cement-based adhesives for flooring. It is much slower to do, but, as the system has been used in one form or another for thousands of years, it cannot be discounted. It is only suitable for fixing onto concrete or sand and cement screeded floors, and is better suited to the traditional thick, unglazed ceramic tile. Commercially, there are all sorts of systems in use, but the only situation where it is likely to be needed in a do-it-yourself situation is where you have a concrete base and there is too much thickness for adhesive fixing but not enough to allow you to lay separate sand and cement screed.

Grouts

These tend to be specialized materials for flooring use and are stronger than wall tile grouts. They also come in standard and rapid-hardening versions and in various colours. Be careful in the choice of colour. As mentioned earlier, floor tile joints tend to go grey eventually no matter what you do. Unless you are prepared to go to the cost of an epoxy grout and spend time keeping the joints really clean, do not count on white or coloured joints staying pristine in the long term. Epoxy grouts are usually only needed if you want to give the joints resistance to something such as oil, acid or alkali. The only situation where they are used in domestic housing is occasionally for kitchen worktops and similar situations.

Tip

If using an epoxy grout always make sure that you clean off properly *as you go along*, as per the instructions. Going off to the pub thinking that you will finish cleaning an epoxy grout off the tiles tomorrow isn't a mistake you will ever make twice.

OPPOSITE: A cool, simple style can look good on a balcony or a patio. But make sure the tiles are frostproof!

CHAPTER 9

Floor Tiling: Setting Out

The rule for setting out floors is the same as it is for wall tiling. If you don't do it properly, it will not look right and you will make more work for yourself in the long run.

Like wall tiling, floor tiling is three-dimensional. A floor has a length, a width and a level. The level is the most important. If you set out the length or width incorrectly the worst you are going to get is a floor that looks bad and is a lot of work to lay. If you get the level wrong you may find that you cannot even finish tiling it.

THE BASIC GEOMETRY

Tiles are flat. If you put four tiles up against each other to form a square panel and keep all the edges of the tiles flush, the panel will still be flat. Extend this principle and you can see that a tile floor can, in theory, only be constructed as a flat plane or as a series of flat planes.

- A floor can be laid flat and level – a level floor.
- It can be laid flat and sloping – laid to falls.
- It can be laid flat and sloping to a corner – laid to falls and cross falls.
- It can even be curved as a series of faceted planes, but only in one direction – barrelled or arched.

A floor is usually laid in just one of these ways. Just

OPPOSITE: A fully tiled luxury bathroom in marble with glass tile inserts. With a multipoint shower and a jacuzzi this is just about the ultimate in bathrooms.

occasionally it may be necessary to use a combination of different methods.

What you *cannot* do with a tiled floor, theoretically, is to curve it in two directions at once, or curve it on the diagonal of the tile, without the tiles lipping.

On most domestic tiling the level will appear to be simple and obvious and in 99 per cent of cases it will be. But there are cases where it can get a little more complicated. A kitchen floor will probably be laid level. If you are laying a patio and want rainwater to run off, you will lay it sloping down to the open edge of the floor (laid to falls). Likewise, you may lay a floor to falls and cross falls (sloping two ways) if you want the water to run into a drain in the corner. In both cases, the floor will be a flat plane that is sloping in one direction, be it to a side or to a corner. A problem will only occur when, for some reason, the floor cannot be laid as a continuous flat plane.

Such a situation might occur when you want the water to run to the middle of a room, to a shower outlet for example. If the concrete has been laid as a series of planes, there is no problem and you simply lay the tiles in the same way and cut the tiles in on the diagonals (this is sometimes called 'enveloping' a floor; draw it out and you will see why). This principle of constructing a floor out of a series of flat planes can cope with the large majority of situations and is the best way of handling things.

However, if the concrete has been laid to a curve, then all sorts of problems crop up. If the curve is in one direction then the floor can be constructed as a series of rows of single tiles, faceted to suit the curve. But, if you have a two-directional curve, you are

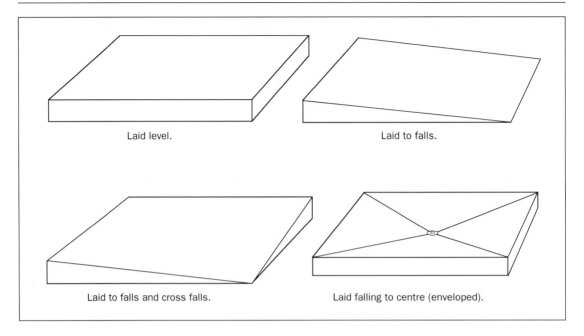

Laid level.

Laid to falls.

Laid to falls and cross falls.

Laid falling to centre (enveloped).

Various types of floor levels.

going to be very limited. Tiles can sometimes be 'humoured in' on a two-directional curve, but only if they are small enough and the joints wide enough, and you will find it difficult to maintain your setting-out lines. If you have a tight curve and a large tile then it can be impossible.

Using a small tile you can 'twist' or 'humour' the floor in more easily. This is a process that has to be done by eye and involves accepting that you are going to have to lay the tiles on a curve and that you are going to have lips. The trick is to try to arrange it that the lips are spread out over as many joints as possible, and are averaged out so that the individual lips are, hopefully, too small to be noticed. A difference in level, which, on a 400mm tile might give a 4mm lip on one joint, using a 100mm tile can be spread over four joints with a 1mm lip on each. If the joint is wide enough this can be an acceptable discrepancy. As you probably have gathered, this is a process that is easier demonstrated than described and is best avoided if at all possible. The point to bear in mind is that the tighter the curve, the smaller the tile you will need to get round it, so you really need to know about it before you even buy your tiles.

CHECKING THE LEVELS

The first thing that a floor tiler does when he arrives on site (other than make the tea) is to establish his levels. This is to make sure that he has sufficient thickness to get his tiles and bed in, and that he will be able to lay a level floor and still meet the adjoining floors without having a step up or a step down.

Just as in the setting out of wall tiles, the idea is to find out if there are going to be any problems so that you can make your decisions on how to get around them. You do not want to find out that your newly laid patio is falling (sloping) the wrong way and your conservatory is going to flood every time it rains.

In commercial work the establishment and maintenance of levels is vitally important, and can be complicated. The various trades work from datum levels given to them by the builder. The builder's surveyor will mark a datum line on the wall of a room and the tiler might be told that his finished floor level is '1,000mm below datum' and the ceiling fixer that his ceiling goes in '1,500mm above datum'. (If you have just worked out that the ceiling height in that room is 2.5m above the finished floor level then you can give yourself a brownie point.)

A tiler starting at one end of a building and a man screeding for vinyl flooring at the other cannot just hope that they are going to meet at the same level in the middle. They have to know that they will. Usually they do!

The first thing is to decide your 'finished floor level'. This is going to be the horizontal level plane to which your floor tiles are going to be laid. In an existing building it will usually be decided for you, as you will have to 'meet the existing levels'. This simply means that the subfloor of the room you are going to tile, and the floors of any adjoining rooms, will be already established and there will be very little you can do about them.

In such a situation, having checked your floor for flatness, you will only need to check the levels at door openings, or any other position where raising the level by the thickness of the tiles and bed might cause problems. Place one of the tiles on a piece of packing to represent the adhesive (the thickness of the bed will usually have been recommended by the adhesive manufacturer, probably in the region of 3mm). Put this down in the relevant position to check whether the thickness you need is going to give you any difficulties. If you are above the adjacent floor you cannot do much about lowering it, but at least you know that you will either need to fit a taper strip to bring the level down or, if possible, ramp up a small area of the adjoining floor to meet it.

Tip

Check a tile thickness by putting it on a flat surface, put a ruler on top of the tile and measure the distance between the surface and the rule. Just looking at the tile edge and measuring that can sometimes be misleading.

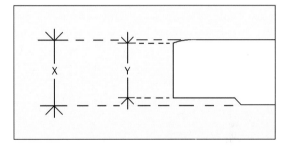

Measuring a tile edge can give a false impression of how much thickness you need to allow for. 'X' is the true thickness, not 'Y'.

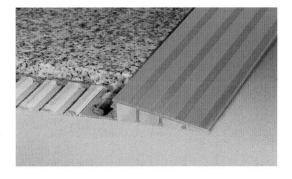

Fitting a 'taper strip' is one method of getting over variations in floor levels.

The horizontal position of everything on a building site is measured from a common datum level.

Datum line

1000   1020

Finished floor level – 1000 mm below datum.

Base level – 1020 mm below datum.

Concrete base

Principles of measuring from a datum line.

If you are fixing in sand and cement then your main concern is to have sufficient thickness to lay the floor. The thickness required for laying will be the thickness of the tile plus the thickness of the bed, and the concrete subfloor should have been 'left down' by the same amount. The purpose of checking the level is to make sure that the concrete is in the right place and that there is enough thickness for you to lay your tiles.

There are various ways that the level can be checked.

Using a Spirit Level and Straight Edge

Probably the simplest way to check the level is to place a block of wood on the floor to represent the thickness of your tile and bed. Place a straight edge on the block (or on the surface of an adjacent floor if that is what you are working from). Pack up the other end of the straight edge with pieces of wood until, by using your spirit level, you know that it is dead level. An assortment of little wood shims is handy for this job. By measuring down from the underside of your straight edge to the top of the concrete you will be able to see what thickness you have for your floor. By moving the first end of the straight edge onto the second packing, levelling the straight edge as before and then repeating this process around the room, you will be able to assess how good the level of the subfloor is. For example, if you need 20mm for your tile and bed and you find at any point that you have only 10mm under the straight edge you know that your concrete is 10mm 'high' and that you are either going to have to raise your finished floor level by that amount or cut the concrete down to give you the 20mm that you need. In older properties it can be surprising just how much a floor can be out of level.

A tiler will usually use a series of tiles temporarily bedded onto the base for the same purpose. These tiles, usually called 'dots', can readily be taken up and rebedded for adjusting to a new level and are not as easily dislodged as packings. Once you are used to it, this method is both quick and accurate.

Using a Laser Level

If you have a laser level the whole thing becomes much easier, and you won't have to do it on your knees. Once you have set up the level and checked it,

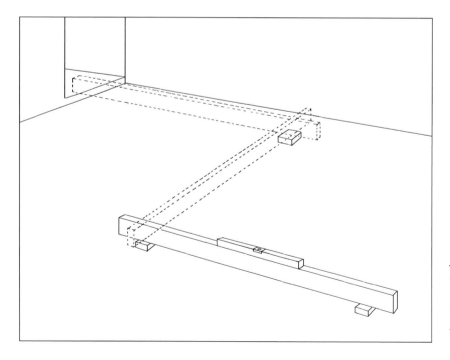

Check a base by establishing a series of 'dots' or packings at the finished floor level. Measuring down from the underside of the straight edge will tell you how accurate your base is.

The tiler establishing his first 'dot' in checking his levels.

Setting up his second 'dot' from the first one. He can then relate that to the level of the floor of the room in front of him.

By rotating a laser level and measuring down from the light beam, a base can be easily checked at any point on the floor.

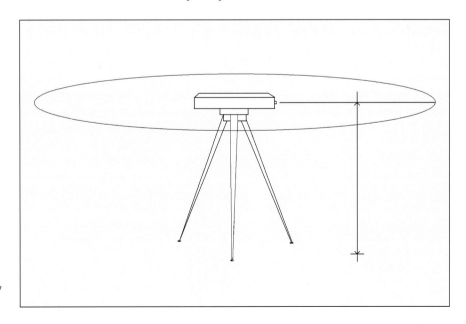

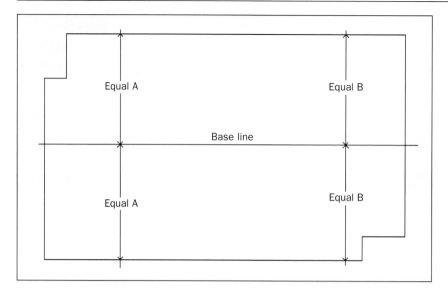

In a simple room strike a true centre line as a base line.

all you have to do is to measure down from the laser beam to any point on the subfloor that you want to check. If all the measurements are the same then you know the subfloor is level. If the dimensions get smaller then you know that your subfloor is rising and vice versa.

ESTABLISHING YOUR LINES

Once you have checked your levels you should know just how you are going to be fixed for thickness, how you are joining up with the adjoining floors and whether or not your floor is going to be flat.

The next stage is the lateral setting out. This is, as it was with wall tiling, the exercise you do to find out the best layout for the tiles. Also, as before, if

Tip
If you are laying the concrete, or screeding, yourself, work accurately. If you have to err, do it on the low side rather than high. It is much easier to build up than it is to chop down. Those extra few shovelfuls of concrete you put in because you didn't want to waste them can involve you in a lot of work if your subfloor is too high.

properly done it will nearly always make the job easier to do. If there are going to be any difficult bits you will know about them before you start and can adjust the setting out to either eliminate or simplify them.

You can do this job single-handedly, but it is much easier if there are two of you. The first thing is to establish the 'centre lines' of the floor. Just like a datum line in wall tiling these are not intended to mark the positions of joints. They are a base to measure from and nothing else. It is important to realize that although often referred to as centre lines, they are often no such thing. They will be true centre lines only on a perfectly regular room.

In a rectangular room, start by finding the middle point of the two shorter walls at each end of the room. If there is a particular wall to which you want your tiles to be parallel, mark the points approximately in the middle, but equidistant from that wall.

The marks are then joined together by tightly stretching your chalk line between the marks, lifting it from the floor as close to the middle as you can and letting it twang back onto the floor to leave a clean, straight line. This is your baseline.

The next stage is your cross line. This goes roughly in the middle of the room and *has to be exactly at right angles to your baseline*. Do not try to establish this by measuring from walls. Just as with wall tiling,

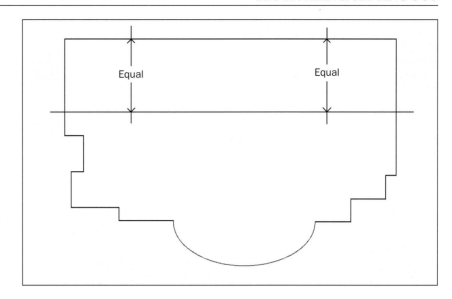

In a room with a more complicated shape it is better to establish your base line parallel to an obvious wall.

Striking a 'baseline'.

Constructing a 3–4–5 triangle from the baseline to establish a cross line.

Repeating the procedure on the other side of the baseline as a check.

Striking the cross line.

we do not want to be working from something that just happens to be there. The usual method is to construct a 3–4–5 triangle. This method has the advantage of being both accurate and capable of being used over any distance. Set squares are not usually big enough, and whilst many laser levels can be set up to project a 90-degree angle, a good tiler will have the line in before you have got the level out of its box.

This method is based on the fact that any triangle that has side lengths in the proportions of three, four and five is a right-angled triangle. It doesn't matter what your units are, they can be feet, yards or metres providing they are all the same. The triangle should be as large as you can comfortably manage. I am going to use metres for the example.

Firstly mark the centre point of your baseline. Then, using your tape measure as a trammel, mark an arc on the floor exactly 4m from this centre point and roughly at right angles to your baseline. Then go back to your baseline and mark a second position on it exactly 3m away from your centre point. With your assistant holding the end of the tape measure on this mark, swing the tape until the 5m mark meets the arc that you drew earlier.

Mark the place where they meet. If you have worked accurately, a straight line drawn through this point and your centre point will be exactly at right

angles to your baseline. Do the same thing on the other side of your baseline. This will act as a check.

All you need to do now is to strike a line with your chalk line through all three points, extending it right across the room. If all three points don't line up something is wrong.

This is the basic setting out for a square or rectangular room. Rooms will come in all shapes and sizes – some will be out of square, some will have curved walls and some will have lots of nooks and crannies, but, with a few special exceptions, the principle is the same from them all.

SETTING OUT THE TILES

You now have a floor with base and cross lines marked onto it which will enable you to set out your tiles accurately. The two lines are the flooring

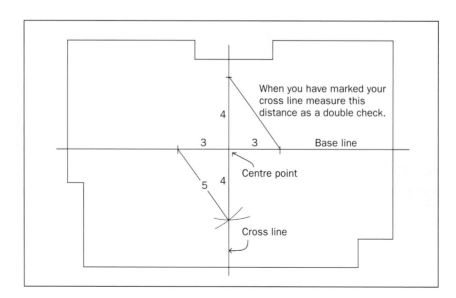

Striking and checking a cross line.

equivalent of the datum line for wall tiling, except that you have two of them, one for the width and one for the length. If the room is a plain rectangle, then it can often be set out simply by laying out rows of tiles, with the joints carefully spaced, on the floor. However, if your room is anything other than quite simple and/or small you may find it easier to make a gauge rather than spend a lot of time moving tiles around, particularly as you will find your spacer pegs always seem to be going missing or getting under the tiles.

Do the setting out of the joints across the width of the room first. This involves seeing how the tile joints are going to be positioned along the *length* of the room.

Just as in wall tiling, use your gauge, in combination with your base and cross lines, to see how your tiles are going to fall with relation to the perimeter of the floor, and any other obstructions that you will have to cut up to. If the floor is a long one you may need to move the gauge across the floor. This is simply done by marking one of the joint positions on the floor and then moving the gauge along until another joint position lines up with it. When you have arrived at the best situation you can, a convenient joint position is marked on the floor. This is your transverse setting-out point. This position should be extended the full width of the

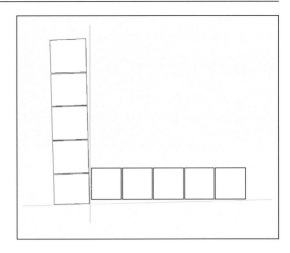

Getting your setting out lines the slightest bit out of square can get you into all sorts of problems. You will be able to work to one line, but not both. And the further you go the worse it will get.

room with a chalk line to form your transverse setting-out line and must be *exactly parallel* to your cross line.

The whole process is repeated for the length of the room, only in this case your setting-out line will be parallel to your base line. You will now have two setting-out lines, one for the length and one for the

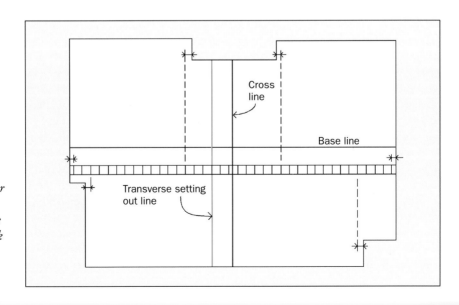

By using your gauge, or laying out tiles, arrive at the best compromise for your cuts and mark your transverse setting out line across the width of the room.

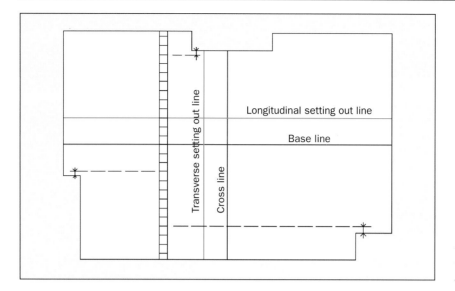

Labels in figure: Transverse setting out line · Cross line · Longitudinal setting out line · Base line

Fixing the position of the longitudinal setting out line.

width. They are lines that represent joints, run the length and width of the rooms respectively, and they should be dead square to each other.

GRIDDING OUT A FLOOR

Most modern tiles are very accurately made and maintain their lines quite well as you fix them. In a small room it is often possible to fix tiles without needing to check the setting out with a gauge lathe as you go along, only a nominal amount of adjustment being needed. However; if you are laying tiles which are at all irregular and need a wide joint, or you are using a wide joint for reasons of appearance, then make a gauge lathe anyway, because you will need to 'grid out' your floor. Wide joints increase the chances of your lines 'wandering' and this makes it advisable to have something to work to. You need to know that you are working square and parallel without having to check measurements every five minutes. This is done by 'gridding out' the floor before you start fixing.

'Gridding out' means marking out with your chalk line a series of parallel lines that actually represent the centre lines of your joints. This is done every five or ten tiles or so. As you lay your tiles, each line has to come on the mid point of a joint and, if it doesn't, you have to adjust your tile until it does. You then

know that, providing you are meeting the lines, your tiles are straight, square and even jointed. It is simply a method of being certain of knowing exactly where your joints should come. If the room is a large one then it pays to grid it out anyway, as all your checking will be done in advance and it will save you both time and worry.

To grid out your floor, use your gauge lathe to extend the setting out by placing it on the floor with a joint centred on your setting-out line. Another joint position a suitable distance away can then be chosen and marked and a new line extended. Keep repeating this until the whole floor is criss-crossed with a grid of parallel lines that represent the centres of your joints. It is important that you take the time and trouble to work accurately. The whole purpose of these lines is to take the guesswork out of the fixing. If these lines are accurately laid out you can confidently tile away knowing that, providing you make

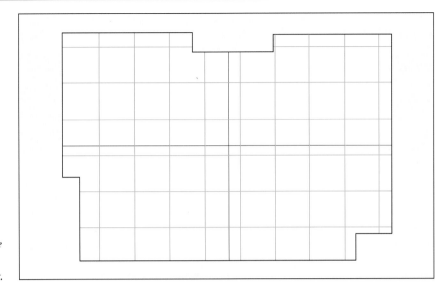

Fully set out floor, 'gridded out' and with base lines and setting out lines shown. From this point on the base lines (shown red) can be ignored. All the other lines represent tile joints.

sure that these lines and your joints coincide, you are not going to get into trouble later.

LAYING THE FLOOR

As mentioned earlier, floor tiles have to be solidly bedded. This means that the layer of adhesive has to be as continuous as you can possibly make it. This is for two reasons. The first reason is that the bed has to support the tile as well as hold it down onto the subfloor. A hollow under a tile, particularly at a corner or edge, creates a weakness that, sooner or later, will give trouble.

The second reason is that floor tiles get a lot of stress. If this is great enough, a tile can 'shear its

bed'. This is a posh term for the tile becoming loose. It does not need a genius to work out that the amount of stress needed to make a tile come loose depends upon how much of it is stuck down. A tile with its entire underside stuck down will require twice the force of one that is only 50 per cent stuck.

For these reasons floor tiles are always solid bedded. This involves using a trowel in which the depth and spacing of the notches are such that, when the tile is bedded in, the ridges of adhesive spread out to fill the gaps between them completely. In addition to that, some tilers like to 'butter' the backs of the tiles as well. This doesn't necessarily give a more solid bed, but it does help if the subfloor is at all uneven

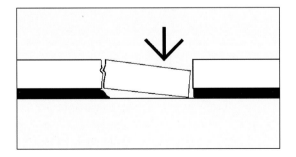

Any serious pressure on a hollow tile will break the tile.

Tip

Some tiles vary in colour from tile to tile, particularly some traditional unglazed floor tiles like terracotta and quarry tiles. When laying these it is important that you take your tiles from more than one box, so that they blend in and you don't get rows or blocks of one shade. Usually five or six boxes is enough, but the more the better. Try to introduce new boxes progressively rather than start a whole new batch.

and it does ensure a good 'take' of the adhesive to the back of the tile.

The first thing is to get your tile boxes laid out on the floor where you can get at them without having to jump up and down all the time but where they won't get in your way too much as you progress.

The next stage is to mix the adhesive. This will usually be a cement-based mortar of one type or another. It may be with or without a modifying resin according to the base you are laying on.

A brief note here about how adhesives set may be helpful. The dispersion adhesives used for wall tiling set by simply drying out. If you put the lid back on the bucket and stop it drying out it will stay usable for months.

Cement-based adhesives, and sand and cement for that matter, set by hydration. This is an irreversible chemical process that starts when you mix in the water. Once it has been mixed, it is going to set and there is nothing that you can do to stop it. The period from when you mix the adhesive, to the time when it starts to set, is called the 'open time' or 'pot life'. This is the time available for you to lay your tiles. The setting process starts with the 'initial set'. This is when the material gradually stiffens up until it can seem quite hard to the touch. However at this stage it has very little strength. It then develops strength until it has fully set. Strength actually develops slowly over quite a long 'curing period' but is usually considered to have fully set when it has sufficient strength to do its job under normal traffic. This will vary with the manufacturer, the type of

adhesive, and the conditions you are using it under and can be anything, from an hour or so for rapid-hardening adhesive, to two or three days for sand and cement and some cement based adhesives.

Stick to the manufacturer's recommendations as to the proportions for the mix. There can be a temptation to put a bit more water in to make it easier to mix and lay, but any water not needed to hydrate the cement has to dry out eventually and extra water means extra shrinkage. The only real guide is that it needs to be soft enough to be easily usable but 'slump free', that is, if you form it into a pile it should stay like that and not 'slump' under its own weight.

Spreading adhesive can be hard work until you get the hang of it. To start with, don't try to lay too much at once. As with wall tiles, this is a two-stage operation. The 'laying on' comes first. This is the process of spreading the adhesive in a good layer on the floor. Decide which direction you want to work in and start at the appropriate setting-out line. Bear in mind that you will need to be able to see the positions of your setting-out lines and any gridding out that you might have done. Spread a good layer of adhesive over a suitable area of the base, with either your floating trowel or the straight side of your serrated float. Sometimes the adhesive is reluctant to stick to the base and will roll up behind the trowel (often a sign that the backing is dusty). If this happens, go back over it, pressing it into the surface until you know you have a good 'take'.

The next step is the 'combing off' when you go back over it with the notched trowel to produce the

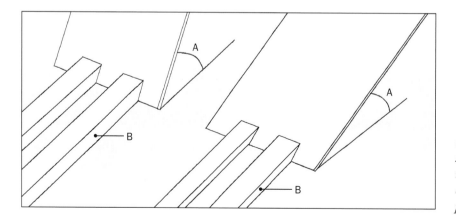

Too narrow an angle (A) when using a serrated trowel can result in the adhesive being too thin for proper bedding (B).

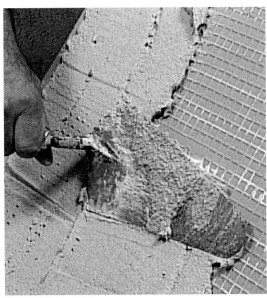

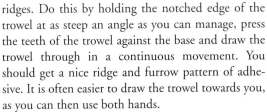

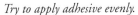

Try to apply adhesive evenly.

Buttering the back of a floor tile.

ridges. Do this by holding the notched edge of the trowel at as steep an angle as you can manage, press the teeth of the trowel against the base and draw the trowel through in a continuous movement. You should get a nice ridge and furrow pattern of adhesive. It is often easier to draw the trowel towards you, as you can then use both hands.

It is important to keep the trowel at as steep an angle as you can. If the angle is too narrow the ridges will be lower, and may not have enough adhesive in them to fill the furrows properly.

Try not to get lumps of adhesive. If you do, clean them off with your pointing or gauging trowel. They can create an uneven thickness and the tiling process is quicker if you do not have to squeeze out excess adhesive and clean it up as you go along. Try to work with your ridges and furrows in a straight line, or at least in a way that keeps the end of the furrow open. As you bed in the tile, the ridge has to squash down to fill the furrow and it helps if you are not trapping air. Don't cover too large an area until you are getting a feel for the process. If you lay more adhesive than you can conveniently fix tiles to, it can skin over and stop your tiles sticking properly.

If you decide that you are going to butter the tile

back (in my opinion this should always be done, no matter what the adhesive manufacturer says), this should be a thin, even layer and is best applied using a pointing or gauging trowel, depending upon the tile size. A wallpaper scraper also does this job well, and isn't as hard on the wrists.

The first tile is bedded exactly on the junction of your two setting-out lines and should be carefully checked to ensure that it is level in both directions and that it is to the correct floor level. This is then extended with additional tiles to form the first row.

Place the first row with the edges of the tiles positioned so that the centre of the joints is exactly on your setting-out line. If you are using spacer pegs insert them as you go along. Press, or tap, the tiles into the bed until the adhesive has spread and filled the furrow. Depending upon the tile size, you may feel a resistance as the tile beds solid. If the tiles are of any size then a rubber hammer is a distinct advantage for this job. If the manufacturer does not state a width, or unless the tiles need wider spacing because they vary in size, use a 3mm joint. Joints narrower than this are not recommended, even if the tiles are dead accurate. You need to be able to get your grout in properly.

Bedding the first tile. Line, level and position are all important, as the first line of tiles extends from this.

Extending the first row of tiles.

The first row of tiles is the most important that you are going to lay. It will make the rest of the job hard if it is out in any way, so take your time, get it right and make sure that you are happy with it. Check that your tiles are flush with each other and that you are working level. If you have grid lines to meet, make sure that any adjustments are made as you go along and that you meet the lines accurately.

Once you have the first row in, carry on with the second row and so forth. Keep checking for both line and level. Use your fingers to check if your corners and edges are flush with the adjacent tiles. It is often easier to feel a discrepancy than it is to see one.

If the tile is not too big, and you are not using spacer pegs, you may be able to level up the surface by 'beating in' the tiles. This is simply going over the face of the tiling beating it with the face of a wooden floating trowel, or a flat piece of wood, to ensure all the joints are flush and the floor is flat. This will tend to throw your joints out and you will have to readjust them.

Try to work in parallel bands in a consistent direction. Try to avoid 'dog-legging' your setting out, that is, changing the direction in which you are working. If you are the slightest bit out of square it can cause problems.

The process of adjustment is the same as with wall tiles. If a tile is not flush with its neighbour, pressing in a high corner will cause the opposite corner to rise. To open a joint, insert a trowel point and twist gently, or insert a trowel blade into the joint and tap the trowel gently to move the tile over. If a tile is slightly high you can often squeeze out any surplus adhesive into the joints, where it can be removed. If it is too low insert a trowel point under the tile, twist slowly until the suction is broken and the tile comes loose. You can then butter the back of the tile with a little more adhesive and refit to the correct level.

Clean any adhesive from the joints, sponge off the floor and leave the floor clean. Finally, scrape any surplus adhesive from the base to leave it clean for you to fix the cut tiles to later.

At this stage don't bother putting cut tiles in unless

Constant checking for both line and level is important.

Filling in the main field.

there is a special reason for doing it; rather, complete everything else to your satisfaction *as you go along*. You do not want to be in a position of deciding that you are not happy with something and then finding that you cannot reach it without disturbing other tiles.

Once all your main area tiles are fixed and you are happy with the result, leave them to set properly. Walking on a floor too soon may not appear to have done any damage, but it can result in tiles coming loose later.

CUTTING IN

There are good reasons for doing the cutting in as a separate process. It is quicker to do these tiles all together. It is also a much slower process than the fixing of the main area. This isn't particularly important with a dispersion wall tile adhesive, as it isn't going to set on you, but cement-based adhesive has a limited pot life. Once you have mixed your adhesive you have to use it before it sets, and if you have mixed enough to do a reasonable area of tiling, then 'cutting in' will slow you down too much and your adhesive may start to set before you have had time to use it all.

The cutting in of floors is a very similar process to

wall tiling; the secret lies in accurate measuring and marking. Measure the opening accurately and deduct from this the width of a joint and an amount for clearance from the wall. Then transfer this to the tile. You can also directly mark a tile from the existing tiles as described in the wall tiling section.

Here is another method of direct marking. It is borrowed from the soft flooring trade, although it is better suited to large tiles. Place a tile *exactly* on top of the adjoining whole tile in the main field. Place another tile on top of this, but overlapping the opening you are cutting into and touching the wall. Mark the line of the other side of this tile onto the top of the first one. This would give you an accurate cut but doesn't allow for your joints and clearance. (In the soft flooring trade materials are usually tight or 'butt' jointed and allowing for joints isn't as important.) So draw another line parallel to this to allow for your joint width and clearance, and then cut to this line. (Alternatively you can put something against the wall to represent the clearance needed and mark to that.) This is a good way of marking 'raking' (tapered or out of square) cuts.

Variations on this method can be used for the accurate marking of more complicated cuts such as

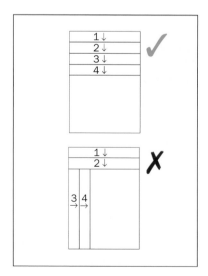

Try to tile in a consistent direction from one side only. Avoid changing your direction of working if at all possible.

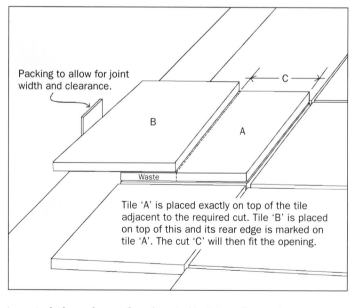

Packing to allow for joint width and clearance.

B

A

C

Waste

Tile 'A' is placed exactly on top of the tile adjacent to the required cut. Tile 'B' is placed on top of this and its rear edge is marked on tile 'A'. The cut 'C' will then fit the opening.

A particularly good way of marking 'raking' (out of square) cuts.

110

Fixing the cuts.

Grouting. As the tile is a large one the tiler is using a soft-faced floating trowel to force grout into the individual joints. This gives a dense joint and leaves less cleaning off to do.

notching around doorposts and other obstructions. In addition, although floor tiles are usually easier to mark up than wall tiles, making templates can still be useful in difficult situations.

If the area you are cutting into is big enough, you can put the adhesive on with the serrated float and fix the tiles in the same manner as the main field. If the area is not big enough to get the float in, then you will have to fix the tile by buttering the back and placing it directly on the base. Using a slight twisting movement, make sure that the cuts are well bedded, flush with the adjacent tiling, and that the joints are properly adjusted.

Tip

Rapid-hardening adhesive can put you under time pressure, so use don't use it until you are confident with the processes involved in tiling. You will need to take your time at first, particularly if you are using heavy tiles. Don't be dictated to by a bucketful of adhesive. You're running the job!

If you are using standard adhesives or sand and cement, once all your cuts are in and you are happy with the floor in all respects, have a day or so off to let the bed set properly. If you're using rapid-hardening material – well, you're just a glutton for punishment.

GROUTING

You should now have a floor which is strong enough to walk on and is ready for the grouting. It is important that the joints are clean before you grout. If anything does get into the joints, sawdust being the most common culprit, vacuum it out before you start. The first thing is to go over the floor and make sure that it is clean and, in particular, that there are no bits of adhesive in the joints that will show once you have grouted.

The grouts used for flooring are different to those used for wall tiling. They are usually stronger and are grittier to the touch. The proprietary grouts available are usually excellent quality and have the advantage of being consistent both in colour and performance.

When grouting, work consistently from one end of the room towards the exit. You do not want to be

Cleaning off.

walking back over a floor that you are grouting if you can possibly help it.

Mix the grout in accordance with the manufacturer's instructions. It should, as in the case with wall tiles, be plastic enough to fill the joints properly. It is very important that the joints are fully filled. It is very easy to grout just the top part of a joint, leaving it hollow underneath. The odd hollow joint may never show itself in wall tiling, but in a floor the chances are that someone will stand on it within a month or two and the grout will come loose and drop down. Apart from the matter of appearance, the grout is a load-bearing part of the floor and if it isn't there to do its job the tile edges will be exposed to damage. If a high-point load is half on a tile edge and half on an open joint, then the tile edge can flake off.

Using a squeegee or a soft-faced floating trowel (the little plastic grout spreaders are not usually substantial enough for grouting floors), work the grout well into the joints. When you are confident that they are fully filled, go back over the area removing as much of the excess grout as you can.

If you are using narrow joints the procedure is just the same as for wall tiles (see Chapter 6). Clean off as much grout as you can with the squeegee and a sponge. There should be very little grout on the face of the tiles and the joints should be left a little over-

full. When the grout has stiffened to the point when it is no longer liquid but has started to become crumbly, the joints should be tooled off using a wooden 'peg' as described for wall tiles, filling in any small exposed voids in the grout at the same time. Do this carefully, section by section, sponging off the floor as you go along. Keep rinsing the sponge in clean water and wringing it out thoroughly. You do not want any surplus water running out of the sponge. Don't try to get the tiles totally clean at this stage. You will not be able to do it without pulling grout out of the joints onto the face of the tile.

When you have got all the joints well filled, evenly tooled off and the tiles at the 'clean but scummy' stage, leave the floor alone until the grout has fully set, usually the next day. You can then clean off the floor properly without any danger of 'pulling' the grout. You should find that the traces of cement come off the tiles with no difficulty. A domestic pan scrub should sort out any odd difficult bits.

GROUTING VARIATIONS

If your floor has wide joints then you have various alternatives. One method is to fully 'tool' the joints using a jointing tool. This is probably the most difficult way of finishing joints and the tiles need to have been accurately fixed with consistent, level joints.

This is done with a 'jointing iron'; this is a metal tool, rather like a bricklayer's jointing tool but with a slightly curved face. These are not easy to buy and tilers often make their own.

This is run up and down the joints until they are smooth and even, any displaced grout then being removed with the sponge. Once the joints have been finished the tiles are cleaned off, taking care not to disturb the grout face. If, for any reason, you have chosen a coloured grout and you want to tool your joints, it might be better to make yourself a wooden tool for the job. It won't produce as good a finish, but metal tools can occasionally discolour joints.

The other method is to sponge-finish the joints. This is done by very carefully reducing the joint to the correct level with a sponge, as part of the cleaning-off process. This leaves a slightly rough joint and a more rustic appearance than is left by tooling. Another, more accurate, way to get the joint surfaces level is to rub over the surface of the tiling with a thin nylon cleaning pad attached to a flat piece of wood. The slight 'give' in the pad allows it to rub the joints down to an even level, just below the surface of the tile. There is a commercial tool, called an emulsifying pad, intended for cleaning epoxy grout from the surface of tiles, which will do the job if you don't want to make your own.

Jointing tool or 'jointing iron'.

Tip

If you decide to mix your own grout then you will need a very fine dry sand without any lumps or coarse particles. Silver sand, sold at builder's merchants, is the usual choice. You will also need a much richer mix than you imagine. Depending on the sand and the joint, between one and two parts sand to one part cement is not too rich for floor tile grouting. The narrower the joint, the richer the mix should be. A guide is equal parts of sand and cement for 3mm joints and up to two parts sand to one part cement for a 6mm joint.

A strong colour on a floor can make a statement in an otherwise bland room.

CHAPTER 10

Floor Tiling – Variations

SAND AND CEMENT FIXING

There are many methods of sand and cement fixing used in the tiling trade, but the majority will be of little interest unless you are building an Olympic swimming pool or a shopping mall in your back garden. For the vast majority of work that needs to be done on a private dwelling house there will be a suitable adhesive fixing system available from someone.

The only occasion when sand and cement might be useful is where the base is either concrete or screed and the thickness needs building up to a degree that stops you using adhesive, but is not great enough to let you lay a separate screed. (A sand and cement screed under about 38mm thick is not usually recommended.)

In many cases it will still be easier to straighten up an uneven floor by screeding with sand and cement that has been modified by adding an SBR (Styrene-Butadiene) resin. This can be 'feathered off' to a very thin layer and still stay stuck down, something that you cannot do with sand and cement by itself, but the resin does add cost and if you are working to a budget then sand and cement by itself is more economical.

Or you might just be more adventurous!

A little background might be useful here. There are two basic systems of sand and cement fixing used for fixing floor tiles. The traditional 'wet bed' system (called the 'sand and cement mortar' system in the British Standard), which is used for thinner beds, and the 'semi-dry' system, which is laid to a greater thickness and is extensively used commercially.

The names used do not mean that the 'wet bed' is

particularly wet, or that the 'semi-dry' method isn't cement and sand mortar, but simply to differentiate between the two systems. Logical it isn't!

We need only concern ourselves here with the traditional cement and sand mortar, or wet bed system. This method is suitable for laying tiles on a bed thickness of between about 15mm and 20mm. This means that you can lay floors to a total thickness of between 25mm and 30mm if you are using a 10mm thick tile.

This involves the following processes:

1. Soaking the subfloor – to stop it sucking water from the bed.
2. Soaking the tiles (if they need it) – for the same reason.
3. Slurrying the subfloor – brushing the subfloor with a mixture of neat cement and water to make sure that the bed sticks to the concrete.
4. Laying the bed – this has to be done to the correct level.
5. Slurrying the back of the tiles – to make sure that the tiles stick to the bed.
6. Laying the tiles and beating them in – to make sure that they are in full contact with the bed.
7. Making adjustments and cleaning off.

The first job is to soak the concrete base with water. This is to stop the concrete taking water out of the bed. This should be given as long as possible to soak in, ideally overnight. When you are confident that no more is being absorbed, then any surplus water should be brushed off.

At this point, if your tiles are porous, you will need

to soak them as well. This only applies to tiles of more than 6 per cent porosity (groups IIb and III are the British Standard classifications). Do this by taking them out of their boxes and completely immersing them in clean water. They need to soak for at least half an hour. With tiles of less than 6 per cent porosity (groups I and IIa), you do not need to do anything.

Whilst any necessary tile soaking is taking place you can mix your 'compo' (sand and cement). You will need a 'soft' sand of the type used for laying bricks. (Sands come in two types in the building trade; the other is 'sharp' sand used for screeding and concreting.) Sands vary hugely from area to area, so check with your supplier if you have any doubts. You will usually get better information from a tile merchant or builder's merchant than you will from a DIY outlet. They know what the tilers are buying. Very fine sands like sea sand or silver sand are not suitable. You will need about 30kg of sand for every square metre of bed at 15mm thick. Whatever you buy in sand you will need about a third of that amount in cement.

Measure out your sand and cement in the ratio of about three and a half parts sand to one part cement by volume. A bucket makes a good measure. (The British Standard says between three and four parts sand to one part cement. But everyone has their own ideas on this point because sands vary so much.)

When you are fixing in sand and cement the first thing that is going to happen is that you will cover up any setting-out marks you have made on the floor, so extend these onto the wall where you can see them. You will also need to be able to check your level as you lay the tiles and the easiest way to do this is to mark a datum on the wall so that you have something to measure down from. Once these have been done you are in a position to get started.

You are going to be working in 'bays', that is parallel strips, towards the exit door. The sand and cement should be mixed dry first to make sure that it is thoroughly mixed and only then should the water be added. You should add just enough water to give a stiff plastic consistency. The mix should lay and consolidate easily, but when you tamp it and rule it off you should not get any free water on the surface.

You have to make sure that the sand and cement bed goes in at the correct level and the easiest way of doing this is to use screed lathes. These are long pieces of wood that are laid temporarily on the floor for you to work off.

These two lathes should be positioned a whole

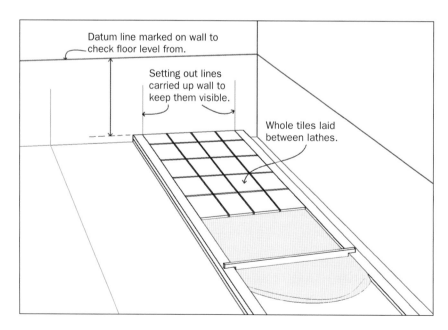

Datum line marked on wall to check floor level from.

Setting out lines carried up wall to keep them visible.

Whole tiles laid between lathes.

Sand and cement fixing: lines and levels.

number of tiles apart, allowing for joints, and the inner edges should line up with your setting-out marks as you will be working in whole tiles between the lathes.

The first lathe should be fixed on the line of the joint between the last whole tile and the cut tile that goes to the perimeter. Slurry two parallel strips of the subfloor about 200mm wide at each side of your working area. These should be far enough apart to give you a good working area but close enough for you to be able to reach both sides of the bay without too much trouble. Lay a run of your compo on top of this and roughly bring it to level. Beat into these your lathes. These should be about 30mm to 50 mm. wide and the thickness should be comfortably less than the total floor thickness you are laying; usually they would be between 20mm and 30mm thick. As you beat them in, check that they are *exactly* to your finished floor level. Make sure that the lathes are secure and scrape off any surplus compo that projects above the surface of the lathes. Cut off any excess compo on the outside of the lathes and then support them with boxes of tiles/bricks to make sure that they don't move once you start laying the tiles. The idea is that we now have an area bordered by the lathes where your bed can be constrained and controlled. Your lathes are to the finished floor level and, in theory, if your tiles are laid flush with the lathes, you can't go wrong.

You now need to be able to lay your compo to the correct level. A straight edge that has been notched so that it fits between the two lathes will enable you to do this accurately. The notches should be slightly less than the thickness of the tile you are using. This will result in the bed being slightly high, enabling you to beat in your tiles properly. Usually about 2mm less than the tile thickness is enough, but if a tile has a deep 'frog' (a hollow space or spaces on the back of the tile), then the notches should be shallower and the bed slightly higher.

Slurry the concrete subfloor in your working area and, whilst the slurry is still wet, lay your compo between your lathes. Tamp it to consolidate it and rule it off by bringing your straight edge towards you. Fill in any voids and level it off with your wood float if necessary. You want a consistent flat surface with no voids or free water.

You now start fixing some tiles. If your tiles have needed soaking they should be taken out of the water a short while before they are needed for fixing, stacked on edge and allowed to drain. You do not want any free water on the tiles.

Slurry the back of the tile and place it on the bed. Tap the tiles into position, making sure that they are bedded properly.

Keep repeating the process just as if you were fixing in adhesive, checking for line, level and joint spacing *as you go along*. There is one difference here from adhesive fixing, which is that you must put in the cut tiles as you go along. As you will probably have set off near a wall you may have to remove one of the lathes to do this. The cutting-in procedure is exactly the same as for the main area. The slurrying and bedding processes should be repeated and the cut tiles carefully beaten in flush with the surrounding tiles.

When you have a suitable area laid, beat the tiles in with a wooden beater or a wood floating trowel to level up the surface to the line of your lathes, finally rubbing over the tiles' surface to bring them to an even surface. Make any final adjustments, remove anything in the joints that might show once you have grouted and clean the tiles off with a sponge and clean water. Do not let any water get into the joints.

As you progress, withdraw and refix your screed lathes and fill in the void they leave with compo, levelling it off with the surrounding bed and fixing

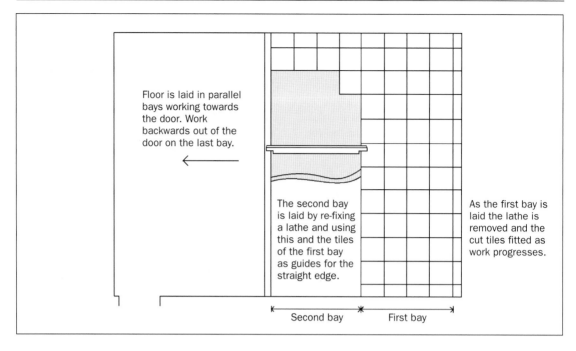

Floor is laid in parallel bays working towards the door. Work backwards out of the door on the last bay.

←

The second bay is laid by re-fixing a lathe and using this and the tiles of the first bay as guides for the straight edge.

As the first bay is laid the lathe is removed and the cut tiles fitted as work progresses.

Second bay ———— First bay

The sequence of laying in sand and cement.

over this in due course. If the lathes have been fixed properly to level you will always be 'ruling off' your bed from either the lathe or from a tile which has been laid level with it. There is no guesswork involved, and you know that your floor will be level.

When you are finishing an area and are finally cleaning up, cut off any surplus bed that projects past the end of your tiles by cutting vertically down the edge of the last tile with the edge of a trowel, scraping off and removing, together with the slurry, any surplus bed. The whole process can then be repeated for the second bay of tiles by refixing one of the lathes and using this and the tiles you have just laid as a guide for your notched straight edge.

The whole method works on the basis that, if your

lathes are fixed to the right lines and levels, the whole area is constrained. If the tiles are then fixed flush with the lathes they have to be in the right position, because there is nowhere else for them to go. All you have to do is to ensure that they are well bedded and the joints are even and straight.

Make sure that the floor has set and is strong enough to take weight before you go on it to grout it. A period of a couple of days is not too long for sand and cement.

The cleaning off and grouting, once the floor has fully set, is exactly as for adhesive-fixed tiles (*see* Chapter 9).

HANDLING TERRACOTTA

It should be stressed that we are talking here about the true terracotta tiles, which are soft, porous and irregular in size. Modern machine-made imitations can be laid in the same manner as any other floor tile.

There is such a variation in the forms and types of terracotta that a system that works with one make can have you struggling with another. For this reason,

---

Tip

Walking on a half-set floor can result in tiles coming loose months later. If you absolutely have to, lay a piece of chipboard on the floor to spread the load and stand on that.

---

you should always follow the manufacturer's instructions. They are the ones who know their materials best. However, the general systems are pretty much the same; the variation is in the detail.

Fixing

Make your gauge lathe and set out as usual, but you will have to fix the tiles by eye whilst using the gauge to make sure that you are keeping the overall spacing correct. The tiles will nearly certainly be too irregular for spacer pegs to be used. Unless the manufacturer recommends a size, don't try to use too narrow a joint – the chances are that the tiles will neither be flat nor regular enough – and check that the fixing system you intend to use is suitable for your particular tiles. Some, particularly the larger tiles, can be so irregular that thick-bed adhesives or sand and cement fixing are really the only practical options. Terracotta can vary a lot in thickness and you may decide to fix your tiles in sand and cement. It can also be quite a weak material and the normal sand and cement mixes can be a bit strong. See what your supplier says about using a weaker mix than is usual for floor tiles. Between four and four and a half parts sand to one part cement is a suggestion.

Always check the tiles for shading. You will almost certainly get a lot of colour variation. Work from as many boxes as you can and mix the tiles well.

Terracotta can be rough and so absorbent that even the cement from fixing or grouting processes can stain it. For this reason it is better to point terracotta, rather than grout it. See what the maker says about pre-sealing the tiles. This is sometimes done to help to protect the tiles during the fixing and pointing processes. It involves sealing the face of the tiles either before you fix them or in the period between the fixing and pointing processes. If you do this, try not to get sealant on the edge of the tiles; it can prevent the pointing from sticking.

If the supplier recommends sealing them after fixing, but before pointing, make sure that the tiles are properly cleaned off first. Leave the tiles to dry thoroughly, clean off any efflorescence that appears and then carefully apply the sealer to the face of the tiling. The idea is that this first coat of sealer will help to prevent the pointing from staining the tile face. The floor is then left for the pointing

to dry thoroughly before the sealing process is completed.

When working with terracotta it is important that you work cleanly. *Never* apply a sealer to tiles that are not really clean, as it can make any dirt or marks nearly impossible to get off later. Most people have enough regrets in their lives already.

Sealing

Whichever method you use, the drying-out process is important because terracotta tiles often contain soluble salts which are brought to the surface of the floor as it dries out. This can form efflorescence, the white fluffy stuff that you sometimes see on old brickwork. You do not want this to start to appear under the sealer.

Once the floor is complete then the maintenance can start. If you have pre-sealed the tiles you will already have decided which sealant system you are using.

There are basically two alternatives. One is the traditional method, which involves working boiled linseed oil into the floor. This has the effect of pre-staining the floor. If the tile surface is full of oil then

Terracotta tiles.

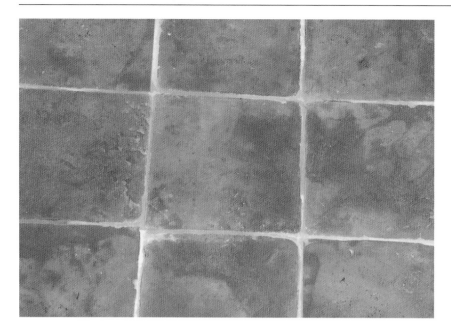

Terracotta can vary a lot both in size and colour.

there is nothing for anything else to soak into. Boiled oil is used as this oxidizes and hardens into a wax with time. The floor is then maintained with wax polishes. It brings a richness of colour and an excellent finish builds up over a period, but it has to be said that it is also both smelly, messy and a long-term project, even if the linseed oil does make your hands nice and soft.

The modern sealants based on synthetic resins are very effective, faster drying, cleaner to use and the manufacturers provide complete systems for both the sealing and maintenance of the floor. They also tend to preserve the original colour of the terracotta better

if you want a lighter coloured floor. Some of the sealant manufacturers are also starting to introduce products that incorporate the more traditional materials in an attempt to get the best of both worlds.

If you are buying terracotta from a source in the UK then the supplier will almost certainly stock a proprietary sealant that will be suitable for their particular tiles. If you decide to go down the more traditional route of boiled linseed oil and wax polishing, then you may have to shop around a little but the materials are still generally available from good DIY shops.

CHAPTER 11

Natural Stones

If you are considering the use of natural stones as tiles it is important that you are doing so for the right reason, and the only right reason is that you love the material. If you think that you will be getting a tougher tile, a harder wearing tile, more stain resistance, a more consistent product, or just about any other property you can think of then you need to understand more about stone.

Natural stones have been used by man for thousands of years, for only two reasons. The first was for structural strength. He needed something strong enough to make his buildings from. The second was for decoration. He needed something to make the buildings look pretty. It is only the second that concerns us.

Although practically any natural stone can be used as a tile, the vast majority will come under the classification of either marble or granite. For floor tiling use you can add limestone and slate to the list. There is no technical reason why these last two materials should not be used for wall tiling, but generally they seem to sell much better for flooring. To help you understand these materials better a brief rundown of the marble trade may help.

The first thing to understand is that, whilst the tiles may be manufactured in a huge, ultra-modern plant in Italy, the materials themselves are not. They are made by an old lady called Mother Nature. She does not run a factory and is not interested in you or your tiling job. She never considered that we might want to stick them to our walls or floors and only makes them for her own purposes. We just happen to find them attractive, and that is the only reason we are using them.

Today, we are so used to consistent, machine-made products that we have come to believe that this is normal. For most of history it was not, and people expected variation both in colour and quality. In natural stones you are going to get some variation and you should be prepared to accept it, at least to a sensible degree.

A peculiarity of the stone market, particularly with marbles and limestones, is that price may buy you beauty but does not necessarily buy you performance. This is counter to all our normal shopping skills. If you spend more money you expect a better product! To some extent this is also true with stone. A good producer will have higher quality standards and will reject a higher proportion of his production and this results in additional wastage and a higher price at the point of sale. But that isn't the end of the story.

Marbles and granites are usually sold 'in the block' by the quarry and bought by the tile manufacturer in that form. Some stones, particularly marbles, are beautiful, but scarce. This means they are in demand and the blocks fetch a high price. Some expensive marbles can also be unsound and quite weak. As a result the 'conversion rate' (the amount of saleable material you are going to get from your marble block) can be very low. If you have paid a fortune for your block and are only going to be able to sell a quarter of it, the price per tile of that particular marble is going to be high.

For this reason, a Bianco Carrara marble tile is usually quite reasonable in price. It is a very sound marble which is available in large quantities, close to the tile producers and has a high conversion rate.

Portoro, a beautiful black marble with gold veins, if you can find it at all in tile form, will be much more expensive and even then the best quality isn't going to get made into tiles, because it fetches a better price in slab form. Giallo Sienna, a heavily veined yellow marble, is both in demand and very weak. You can pay a lot for it and it will still not be as durable as many cheaper marbles.

So remember that the strength, hardness and durability of the tile are properties of the individual marble and have little to do with the price you are going to pay. The factors that affect price are scarcity, demand, the conversion rate and the cost of producing the tiles. Strength or durability only come into it if they start to affect demand. (This is a polite way of saying that if a block is such rubbish that nobody wants it, then it will be cheap.)

Natural stones of any type are not always totally solid. They can have veins in them which are sometimes softer and less solid than the main body of the material. Sometimes there are actual voids. This is particularly so with marble. When the solid material is cut into thin slices, these are exposed. The more friable and open-textured portions show up as 'vents' or faults in the material. These are filled, usually with synthetic resin, whilst the marble is still in sheet form and before it is cut into tiles. These can sometimes show as a slight difference in texture on the face. These are an integral part of the material and some of the most decorative and desirable marbles will need the most filling. It is important to understand that, with natural stones in general, and marble in particular, such cosmetic treatments are normal and always have been.

Tip

If you want to see just how much a piece of marble has had its face 'filled' before being polished, turn it over and look at the back. This will give you some idea of what the face looked like before filling. Only the seen face is usually filled.

MARBLE

A quick note here on 'marble' and 'limestone'. To the geologist these are very specific terms. They are both made from the same material, calcium carbonate, but limestone is a sedimentary rock whilst marble is metamorphic. Marble is simply a limestone which has been subjected to heat and pressure until it takes a crystalline structure. This makes a big difference to its properties. As a rule, marble is harder, denser and finer textured than limestone.

Unfortunately, for the geologist as well as the marble trade, things are not as simple as that. Mother Nature's finishing shop is not all that efficient. Some limestones have had practically no pressure, which makes them very soft and porous. Some have had a fair amount and are nice, dense materials, much loved as building stones. Some get pressure to a point where the crystals start to form, but the process is never completed. At the top end of the range there are the true marbles which have a totally crystalline structure. From this, you will have been able to gather that there is no real dividing line between a limestone and a marble, the divisions being largely arbitrary.

However, within the trade there is a general acceptance that, if it takes a polish, it can be called marble, if not, it is limestone. It is pretty much down to the supplier to decide what he is going to call it and there are many classic 'marbles' that are, in fact, limestones. Conversely there are materials which do take a good polish but are still sold as limestones. However, as a general rule, marbles are harder, denser and easier to maintain than limestones. To paraphrase Mark Twain, 'Marble is limestone with a college education.'

LIMESTONE

Here we mean the true limestones, the ones which will not always take a polish and are generally softer and more absorbent than the true marbles. Popular for flooring, some of these are very attractive and are often used when a stone-like appearance is needed, but with a surface that is easier to clean than most sandstones. They vary in colour from being practically white through to the rich browns.

Moving a block. A Perlato Sicilia marble quarry in Sicily.

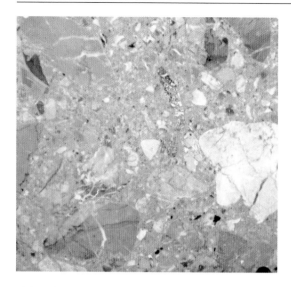

A 'conglomerate' or reconstructed marble.

Whenever a material becomes fashionable people want to add it to their range of products in order to maintain sales. They may be well intentioned but dealing in natural stones of any kind calls for a degree of specialized knowledge. Limestones can vary hugely in hardness, density and absorbency and, as with any natural stone, try to buy from someone who understands the subject or at least has been selling it for long enough to know what *not* to sell. Remember that chalk is a limestone too, but I wouldn't want it on my floor.

There are some first-class limestones available, but some of the materials on the market are both soft and absorbent and can also be difficult to look after and keep clean. Sealers are available, but it is difficult to make the tiles totally stain-proof without altering the character of the surface. If you are fancying a pristine white limestone floor in your kitchen, and are also into serious cooking, then bear in mind that you will probably never get the olive oil stain out, particularly if you choose the wrong one.

CONGLOMERATES

The only reason a marble or granite tile is in the shop is because the stone itself is capable of being cut to the size and thickness required. There are many marbles which, although beautiful, will never be sold in tile form simply because they fall apart if you try to cut them thin enough. Also, because Mother Nature doesn't make tiles, only rocks, a particular quarry can run into a bad area and a marble which has been sound for a hundred years can suddenly have serious quality problems.

A way around these difficulties is the 'conglomerate' or reconstructed marble tile. The smaller material from the quarry is graded, mixed with either cement or a resin and then formed in a mould to produce a block. This is then cut into tiles just as if it was solid marble. This system gives the quarry an outlet for the smaller material which otherwise might not find a market and, because the conversion rate is very high, it is a way of making the weaker marbles less expensive. It is also a method of producing a tile in a material which would simply not be available otherwise.

I want to make it clear that I am using the word 'conglomerate' to describe tiles made in a particular way. Geologists use it differently. Mother Nature does produce her own conglomerates and some marbles are, in fact, natural conglomerates.

GRANITE

Just as with marble, granite is a different thing to the geologist than it is to a mason. To a mason it is a general term for a range of hard igneous rocks that will take a polish. Although granite is cut and polished in the same way as marble, it is in a different league when it comes to hardness and consistency, and it is the greater cost of working it that accounts for most of its higher price. Granite can be very hard indeed, and this, together with its chemical make-up, means that it is also much less liable to its polish being damaged. It has tremendous resistance to weathering and this has made it the material of choice for monuments and memorials for over 4,000 years. It is usually quite consistent in texture and colour (but not always – there are some quite 'wild' granites). It does not have the same amount of veins and vents that so typify marble, but it does have some absorbency and can still be stained, although much less readily than with marble. For the tiler, its toughness makes granite much more difficult to cut. With the exception of a few obscure stones such as quartzite, granites are the hardest of all masonry materials.

SLATE

This is another group of highly variable materials. They differ from most of the other common stones that are available as tiles, in that they are laminar materials. This means that they were originally laid down as sediments in thin layers and they can be split or 'riven' into thin sheets on the lines of those layers. In this form they were, and still are, commonly used as roof tiles. Slate resists the passage of water very well and has a good resistance to chemicals. (One of its other uses, particularly in Yorkshire, was for making vats for brewing beer.) It is both weather-resistant and highly durable – as an example, good snooker tables still have slate beds.

Slate was used as a writing surface for hundreds of years and this gives a clue to another property, at least of some slates – they mark easily. This is not a problem as the marks are usually easy to remove, but to keep a black slate floor mark free can involve very regular washing. Slate can also be stained by oil; it is therefore common practice to seal slate after laying as this makes the maintenance easier. A hundred years ago it was common to oil slate as a way of finishing it. In effect, it was a way of making it resistant to staining by pre-staining it – not usually recommended today. It was a smelly, messy process and nowadays there are better materials available for sealing the surface.

Slate is usually available in a bigger range of sizes than other natural stones and is also, depending upon the manufacturer, sometimes available in two finishes.

The first finish is 'riven' – which is the slightly

Today, slate comes in a variety of colours.

A green slate tile; the right half has been sealed.

rough, undulating surface that is left when a tile is riven, or split, from the block. The other is a smooth, 'fine rubbed' or 'honed' finish. This is produced by grinding the face of the slate finer and finer in exactly the same way as marble or granite. The only difference is that slate will not take a polish and is not available in polished form. Until recent years the only slate generally available came from the UK and this meant that, with the exception of Cornish, most slates tended to be a rather pleasant subdued black, green or purple. Today, there is a much greater range of colours available as supplies come in from places abroad; China and India are both large producers of slate.

CHAPTER 12

Tiling with Natural Stones

The historical image of marble as a luxury cladding and flooring material has been due, as with most things in life, as much to its cost as to its beauty. The Romans were happily shipping marble around their Empire 2,000 years ago, and marbles and granite have always been available to the wealthiest in society. However, the cost of working and transporting the material meant that, even for the well-to-do, it was a dream, and for the man in the street, something to be marvelled at. The cost of transporting such thick materials also meant that, even if you were very rich, you would usually be limited to materials that were obtainable locally.

With the Industrial Revolution came the development of the technology to cut marble into slabs economically, using powered saws, together with lower transport costs. This made them much more affordable, but, until quite recently, they were still luxury materials that were out of the reach of most people. Tiles are now made in automated factories, at a thickness that has made them much more economical to transport. Container shipping has greatly reduced shipping costs in real terms and natural stones such as marble and granite can now be bought at prices which, whilst still not cheap, at least make them affordable for that special situation. The advent of adhesive fixing systems has also simplified the fixing of many of these materials and although some special equipment is still needed, they can now be successfully fixed by a non-professional.

Traditionally, the use of marble and similar stones was a completely different trade from that of a floor and wall tiler. Even within the stone trade itself the skills were, and still are, divided into those of stone

mason, who specialized in structural work, and the marble mason, who is more involved with non-structural, cladding work, and needs special knowledge of polishing. Even within today's wall and floor tiling trade, when all the materials are available pre-packaged and ready for fixing, some specialized knowledge of the materials is needed if the job is to be well done.

The most common natural stones used for wall tiling are marble and granite. With a few rare exceptions, it was not possible until quite recently to fix these materials to walls using adhesive. Until the technology arrived to economically cut the tiles thin enough, marble and granite were simply too heavy to be stuck to a plaster or rendered backing without the danger of pulling it off the wall. Most materials were a minimum of 20mm thick and had to be fixed to the structure mechanically with metal cramps and ties. Occasionally thin tiles might be specially made, but it was a slow and expensive process. Suddenly diamond blades became much more economical and available, and, with the advent of computer-controlled saws, it became possible to produce thin tiles practically automatically. Today, in the most modern plants, the majority of the staff seem to be doing the inspection and quality control. The manufacturing process is nearly completely automated.

The range of stones available as floor tiles is greater than that for wall tiles. In many cases there is no reason for this. Some materials, such as slate, have traditionally been used for flooring and tend to be sold primarily for that purpose, although it is perfectly satisfactory for walling. The only qualifying factor is weight. Some materials have to be produced at a thickness which makes them too heavy for fixing in adhesive as wall tiles, at least in most situations.

USING NATURAL STONES AS WALL TILES

Backings

A marble or granite tile can be between a quarter and a third heavier than a ceramic tile of the same thickness, and natural stone tiles will often be thicker than the same sized ceramic tile, particularly in the smaller sizes. Because of the extra weight involved it is even more important that the backings that you are going onto are strong enough. As a guide, your tiles shouldn't be more than about 10mm thick if you are fixing onto a well-fixed plasterboard or 6mm or 7mm if the plasterboard has been skimmed with plaster. This may seem odd, but it is because tile adhesive sticks better to plasterboard than a skim coat of plaster does. (You may be able to stick to the skim coat, but if that comes away your tiles will still drop off.)

If you have any choice in the construction, then some of the proprietary backing boards are stronger than plasterboard. If you are using one of these, check what the manufacturer says about the maximum weight they can carry and what the recommended fixing system is.

The ideal backing for a marble or granite tile is a good sand and cement render onto a brick or block wall. Properly done, this is the strongest of the in situ backings and can be incredibly strong. Anyone who has ever had to chop off a well-fixed tile job from the 1930s or 1940s will be able to vouch for this.

The Materials

Marble and granite need more care in fixing than ceramics for very good reasons. In most cases, they are going to be much more expensive. So if you make a mistake, either in the fixing, or in the cutting, it is going to cost you more. They also have completely different attributes to ceramics and if you treat them in the same way you can permanently damage your tiles. Because the range of properties of natural stones is so big it is not possible to list everything that you might come across, but you should be aware

of the general properties so that you know what *not* to do.

Firstly, the polish on the vast majority of marble and granite tiles is not a synthetic applied finish. The actual material is polished in the same way that a diamond is. It is ground finer and finer, each grinding process improving on the last one. The final shine is produced by using acids to chemically remove the last microscopic scratches. This means that the polish has no protection and, as marble is quite soft, it is also easy to scratch.

Marble is also absorbent, although this varies in degree from type to type. Practically any liquid will be absorbed into marble and if it is one that will not evaporate completely, or can leave residues behind, it will stain the tiles. Marble will also stain from behind, travelling right through the thickness of the tile quite quickly. As some adhesives contain resins which can stain permanently, you have to be certain that the one you are using is suitable for the job. Always check this with your supplier if you are fixing marble or granite. Even an adhesive that is suitable for marble may produce some temporary discolouration as the water from the adhesive soaks into the tile, but this will disappear as the tiling dries out.

Oil and grease are the big issues with regard to staining, particularly animal or vegetable oils. These will stain marble permanently and, although there are some techniques for removing stains, these are specialized and often only work well on the lighter mineral oils. Once oil has oxidized in the marble it will be practically impossible to remove. As many cosmetics contain vegetable fats or oils, if you are going to tile a dressing-table top, then special precautions will be needed.

Another characteristic of marble is that many are translucent and any variation in the colour of the backing can show through onto the face, changing the colour slightly. If you are using a light-coloured tile and a dark adhesive, the lines of adhesive can show through and create an unsightly pattern on the finished tiling. If you have any doubts at all, use a white adhesive if you are using a light tile. As a matter of routine you should give a light coat of the adhesive over the whole of the back of the tiles as you fix them. This ensures that there is at least a consistent colour behind the tiles.

Another property of marble is that it is made of calcium carbonate and this doesn't like acids of any kind. Even a mild acid will damage the polish on marble and can do so quite quickly. For example, carbonated drinks can burn the polish from marble and, although your favourite bistro might have marble tables that appear to be unmarked, these will usually have been specially lacquered, or will have a coarser, 'fine-rubbed' finish that doesn't show marks as easily.

There are sealers available that you can apply to the face of natural stones to give them some resistance to chemical attack and/or staining, but don't expect miracles from them. They are not going to make your tiling bulletproof. When using materials as traditional and beautiful as marble there really is no substitute for looking after it properly.

Fixing

The basic techniques of tiling with marble tiles are no different from those of any other wall tiles. Follow the instructions given in Chapter 6, bearing in mind that the material is different and that there are some extra things to know and extra precautions to be taken.

Let's assume that you are happy with your backings and the colour and type of adhesive you have decided to use. You have checked your tiles and have decided your joint width.

You have done your setting out, have lathed the job up, and are ready to start fixing.

Fix the tiles exactly as you would any other wall tile, but with the following qualifications.

Unless you are certain about the properties of your tiles remember to take the precaution of coating the whole of the back of the tile with adhesive. Take your time and work methodically and, until you are happy that you have the hang of things, take it slowly. If you are using a polished marble, take every precaution you can to avoid scratching the tiles. Don't let any metal tools come into contact with the face of the tiles and try to avoid touching the tiles with anything that can scratch them throughout the whole fixing and grouting process. Even a pan scrub can scratch some marbles.

Clean off as you go along, using a damp sponge. Don't leave any adhesive on the face of the tile. You do not want to have to try to remove anything from the tile face once it has set, particularly a cement-based adhesive.

If you are using a square-edged tile as opposed to a bevel-edged one you may want to beat in the face of the tiles to keep their edges as flush as possible. If you do, use a flat piece of very soft wood and make sure that it is clean.

One characteristic of all natural stones is that they are heavier than ceramics. This means that they tend to slide when used as wall tiles and therefore the use of spacer pegs is essential. It also means that, if you do too many courses at once, the lower pegs can get trapped by the pressure and can be difficult to remove. Pulling them out with pliers can sometimes damage the edge of the weaker marbles, particularly with square-edged tiles. If in doubt, take it slowly and don't fix the higher courses until the lower ones have set enough to carry the weight above without moving.

Cutting

Once you come to the cutting then you are going to need an electric tile saw, as there is no other way of cutting these tiles effectively. If you have a lot of cutting to do it will probably pay you to buy or hire one. If you have only a few, then marking them up and getting your supplier to cut them for you is probably the better bet.

Getting Around Corners

When you come to going around corners then the corner trims that are used with ceramic tiles work fine with marble and granite and are probably the best solution for the vast majority of jobs.

Tip

If you do get any adhesive on the face of the tile and you have no choice but to clean it off later, use something that is softer than the tile. A piece of soft wood or, for small bits, a fingernail. Do it wet and, with cement-based adhesives, as soon as possible. If you are using a dispersion adhesive, these will usually soften if you keep them damp for long enough.

Tip

For finally cleaning down marble or granite a wash leather with clean water is as good as anything. Don't use chemical cleaners or polishes unless you know they are safe.

There are other ways of getting around corners with natural stones. The use of a butt joint is by far the most practical solution if you don't want to use edge trims. This is exactly the same process as if you were using a round-edged or glazed-edge ceramic tile. The finished edge of the return tile 'masters' the cut tile to the wall face.

The problem is that a butt joint will involve polishing some of the tile edges. This will generally be a non-starter in the case of granite, as the material is simply too hard for it to be done economically without special equipment. But you may be able to get your supplier to polish some for you.

With care, the edge of a marble tile can be finished to a reasonable standard. Use a wet and dry abrasive paper wrapped around a wooden block. Start with a grade just coarse enough to remove any machine marks left from the manufacturing process. Using the paper wet, keep the block square on the edge of the tile and run it evenly up and down the edge until you have as even a finish as that grade of paper can produce. Keep the pressure constant and try to avoid creating any distortions. Then use the next grade up of paper to remove any scratches from the first paper. Repeat this process using finer and finer grades of paper until you get to quite a high sheen, usually about a 600-grit paper. At this stage, a marble

polisher would use chemicals to finish the polish. These can be dangerous and are not usually available to the general public.

However, quite a good finish can be obtained by using a proprietary marble polish to give the final gloss. On no account use any polish not intended for use on marble. Marble polishes are based on synthetic resins that don't soak into the material, and therefore don't stain it. Once you have some tiles with polished edges you can treat them just as if they were ceramic tiles with glazed edges.

If you do want to use a butt joint and do not want to be involved yourself in polishing edges, check if your supplier will be able to polish them for you and what they would charge. If they have the right equipment they may be able to do them quite economically.

Other methods of getting around corners do exist, but we are getting into the realm of the marble mason rather than the tiler. These are the various forms of mitred corner. A full mitre is usually avoided in the masonry trade as it leaves a very weak corner that is far too easy to damage. If a corner is not at 90 degrees, a 'mason's mitre' is used, which is simply a variation on a butt joint.

There are other ways it can be done; one is the 'bird's beak' mitre. In a bird's beak, a bevel is taken off the back of a tile that has its edge polished. The square edge of the tile is left in place to give strength. When two such tiles are butted together a V-shaped joint (the bird's beak) is left. This can give a nice feature to an external corner and is fine on a continuous run of angle, but if you imagine the complications of doing it to the notched tiles to the corners of a window, you will realize that it is only for the

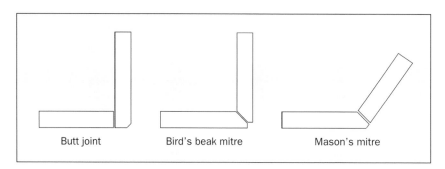

Butt joint   Bird's beak mitre   Mason's mitre

Getting around corners with natural stones.

hardiest of DIY enthusiasts. In granite I wouldn't advise anyone to try it.

Grouting

The grouting of marble and granite follows the same procedure as for ceramic tiles with some provisos. Check with your supplier that the grout you are using is suitable for the tile. If you are using square-edged tiles take particular care in finishing the joints as any variation tends to be more noticeable with square edges than it does with bevelled edges. Granites are usually hard enough to stand up to most things, but if your tiles are marble do not use anything that can scratch the tile face. Use a soft squeegee, a sponge and/or a piece of cloth for grouting and cleaning off.

Be very cautious if you are thinking of using coloured grout. It should not be a problem if you just want to match the colour of the marble, but marble is absorbent and easily stained. If you have any doubts at all, do a small trial as a test before you commit yourself to doing the whole job.

USING NATURAL STONES AS FLOOR TILES

Bases

In the floor tiling section I mentioned that there is a trade-off between the strength of the tile and that of the subfloor. The reason that I am mentioning it again here is that many natural stones, and marbles in particular, are hugely variable in strength. This variation is not just between types of marble, but it can be from batch to batch. (Mother Nature is at it again.) A concrete subfloor is not usually a problem. If the tile is well fixed it is only providing the wearing surface; the concrete provides the strength. However, timber floors should be prepared on the assumption that the tile itself is not going to impart much strength to the system and should be made as rigid as possible.

Just as with ceramics there is no magic formula that I can give you. So when laying onto timber subfloors, take every precaution that you can and do your preparation as carefully as possible. Even if a timber subfloor is perfect it is still better to use a flexible polymer modified cement-based adhesive. The extra flexibility these give, and their higher bond

---

> **Tip**
>
> Always look at the back of a travertine tile, to see how many holes there are. It can give an indication of quality – you don't want to be buying too much fresh air. If nothing else, you might impress the salesman!

---

strength, can be a distinct advantage. Tell your supplier what you are fixing and what you are fixing onto and ask for his recommendations.

The Materials

Just as with ceramics, strength becomes much more important when fixing onto floors and whatever you use has to be strong enough to stand up to the stress and hard enough to take the wear. You can never be totally certain as to the strength of any natural stone but as a general guide:

- Granites are both hard and consistent.
- Slate is tough, usually very durable, but not particularly hard.
- Marbles and limestones can be very variable both in strength and hardness, and these properties can vary from type to type and from batch to batch.

The strength of marble in particular can vary tremendously from type to type. Some marbles have two and a half times the compressive strengths of others and five times the tensile strength.

To confuse the issue even more, some granites have lower compressive strengths than some marbles, but because they are more consistent and much harder they will usually perform better as flooring. Even if you acquaint yourself fully with the properties of marbles the whole subject is a moving target, because, as noted above, the quality of a marble can vary from batch to batch. So apply the same rule that you would for any other purchase you might make. Buy from someone who knows the trade and ask their advice.

There is one class of marble which deserves special mention because this type does differ from the general run of material – the travertines. This is a range of very distinctive marbles varying in colour

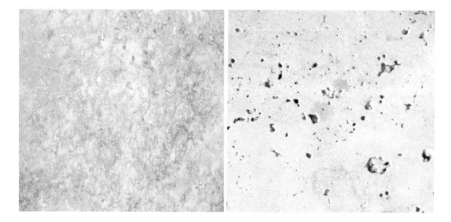

The same area of a travertine tile (about 150mm square) from the front and from the back.

from pale cream to dark brown. They have been popular since Roman times and are still widely available today. What distinguishes them is that they are literally full of holes. It is these which give the marble its distinctive character, but, in some of the travertines, they also weaken it considerably.

The holes are not usually visible because they are filled with cement or resin before the tiles are polished. This is usually done to match the colour of the marble, but occasionally might be in a contrasting colour to show the distinctive nature of the material to more advantage. Travertine will always be fine for wall tiles but be careful if using it on floors, particularly for heavy use. The amount of voids varies from batch to batch and the holes that have been filled are only the ones that could be seen at the time of filling. There will always be more just below the surface and these can be exposed as the floor wears. Some people quite like this effect but, if dirt gets into holes in a cream filled travertine, it can be quite disturbing if you are not expecting it.

Many marbles and granites are sold with a mirror polished surface, usually referred to as an 'acid' polish from the method by which it was done. These finishes are fine for walls, but if you are using them for flooring make sure that you are happy with this finish. If they 'matt down' with wear there is little possibility of you being able to restore them to their original condition. The polishing systems used in a marble works are not available to the general public and the applied sealers and proprietary marble polishes do not have quite the same effect.

If you are using granite it will usually be hard enough to stand up quite well and smooth slate tiles are supplied with a fine rubbed surface anyway. But highly polished marble used in a high traffic area that is subject to outdoor shoes can loose its polish and show 'traffic lanes'.

I personally like marble floors to have a 'fine rubbed' or 'honed' finish. This is a very fine eggshell-like finish, often used for finishing marble statues. It has a wonderful feel and character, which, although it doesn't give the brilliance of colour that a high polish does, has a warmth and softness of appearance all of its own. It is also very like the patina that a marble floor will develop naturally after many years of wear. Which makes it easier to look after!

When using any natural stone for flooring, be prepared to accept the material for what it is. The textures and patinas that develop over time are the great beauties of natural materials and are qualities for which they have been valued over the ages. Get it right and your floor might still be giving pleasure in 200 years, and will never have been out of fashion in all that time.

Fixing

Just as with wall tiling, although the basic system for floors is no different when fixing natural stone tiles, techniques differ slightly from those used for ceramics. This is due to the properties of the individual materials and, as stated earlier, mainly involve knowing what not to do.

Ceramic tiles are generally reasonably tough and,

with the exception of a few materials such as terracotta, providing they have been well fixed and grouted there are not many things that can cause you serious problems. At least none that cannot be remedied. This is not the case with some natural stones. They are all absorbent to some degree, so keep oils of any kind away from all of them. Other than that, they all have their own particular properties.

The usual precautions need to be taken. Check with your supplier that the tile is right for the situation and the amount of wear it is going to get. Make sure that the adhesive and grout you are buying are suitable both for the material and where you are going to use it. Let's start with the easiest first.

Granite

Although there are exceptions to every rule, generally granites can be treated pretty much as you would a ceramic tile.

If the tiles are square-edged then take the precaution of 'beating them in' to eliminate lipping. Take care to adjust and clean the joints as you go along. The only special precaution you need to take is to make sure that the whole of the back of the tile is coated in adhesive. Although this should be normal practice for flooring anyway, there are some granites that can show water staining from the back when they are fixed. If you are using a resin-modified adhesive there is just a faint chance that the staining could become permanent. It would only be slight and if the whole of the back of the tiles is coated you won't even notice it, but if you have missed bits these could show up as lighter patches when the floor dries out.

Slate

As most slates resist the passage of liquids very well you are less likely to get any staining from the back. Some slates do show a quite dramatic heightening of colour when they are wet and this effect can be used to advantage by sealing the floor to bring the colour up. (More about sealants later.) What you do not want is for this effect to happen by accident.

If resins come into contact with the face and are allowed to dry they can cause faint watermarks that can be difficult to remove, so clean off the tiles properly as you go along.

Slate is often available with a riven face. Riven

materials have to be fixed in a different manner to other tiles. This is because the plane of the tile's face is decided by the line of layers formed by the sediments as they were laid down. These were never dead flat and so neither is the tile face. As the tile edges follow the line of the tile face, they are not going to be straight either. This means you are not going to be able to lay the tiles without lips no matter how much you try. If you are going to have lips then there are two precautions that you can take. The first is to try to hide them. This is done by increasing the joint width. The tiles may have been sawn accurately enough for you to use a 3mm joint, but this might make a lip look very obvious. Increasing the joint width to 10mm would make it much less so. The size you make the joint is a matter of judgment and will depend entirely on how much variation there is in the line of the tile edges. This in turn depends on the size of the tile, the type of slate and the particular batch the tiles were made from. Between 6mm to 10mm would be quite usual and for very large tiles it could even be more.

The second precaution is to make sure that the lips are as small as possible. The only way you can do this is to 'average' the lips as best you can. This is simply a case of adjusting the tiles as you fix them to give the best result. If you think one corner is too high, you

A clean, well-sealed slate floor.

tap it down to a lower level. The opposite corner will come up, but hopefully not enough to give you problems. If two opposite corners are high and the other two are low, then rotating the tile through 90 degrees might do it. It is all a matter of choice and judgment and a little bit of luck.

One of the properties of a riven material is that the cement from the grouting process gets into very fine grooves in the face of the tile. During the grouting process, when you are cleaning off the tiles and are at the 'clean but scummy' stage you might find that you are having difficulty getting all this residue out. Use a very clean sponge, rinse and squeeze it out every time you use it, and change your water regularly. You may not manage to remove it all, but you will be able to get it to a stage suitable for chemical cleaning later when the grout has set.

On smooth tiles, if the cleaning off has been done properly, any grout residue left on the face of the tile will be powdery and quite easy to clean off. Once into the crevices of a riven finish it is another matter

Grout, and sometimes dirt from cleaning, can get into grooves in riven slate and can be very difficult to remove if it gets sealed in.

and can be quite difficult to get out completely. However, slate, and a few other natural stones, mainly granites, have the advantage that they usually resist acids quite well, and this fact is used by some of the cleaners that are sold to get over this problem. These work by reacting chemically with the grout residues and dissolving them. They can then be rinsed off with clean water. Although these cleaners are not as powerful as some of the trade materials, it goes without saying that, because they are sometimes based on hydrochloric acid, they have to be treated with respect. Always check that they are suitable for the particular material that you are using and follow the instructions to the letter. Another point – never, ever use an acid-based cleaner on marble or limestone.

Marble

If you are contemplating using marble floor tiles it is important that you choose one which has been finished in a manner you will be able to maintain in the particular area that you are putting it in. Marble comes in various finishes from a glass-like 'acid' polish to a quite rough-textured 'tumbled' or grit-blasted finish. If the tiles have a very high acid polish it is not usual to seal them. Such a polish is difficult to maintain on floors as it tends to matt down with wear, and no amount of polish applied later can replicate the finish. Acid-polished marble floor tiles are usually best laid in places where vulnerable areas can be protected by rugs or carpets.

The best finish for most floors is the 'honed' or 'fine-rubbed finish'. This has a slight sheen rather than a shine and roughly approximates the finish that a floor would develop naturally under foot traffic, and is much easier to maintain.

Once you are happy with your choice of tiles these can be treated much as any other floor tile with respect to the basic fixing techniques, but you will still have to take all the precautions against scratching and staining that are given in the wall tiling section. Always give the back of the tile a continuous coat of adhesive and, if you are using a light-coloured tile, or one that is in the slightest bit translucent, use the white version of the adhesive. If you are using a white adhesive and a grey grout, make sure that any excess adhesive is thoroughly cleaned out of the joints as you go along. Any bits you miss will show up far more once you have grouted.

Limestone

Every note and comment that applied to marble also applies to these but with a few special recommendations. A few of the limestones can also be extremely absorbent, to a degree that they can be marked quite readily by the materials used for fixing and grouting. As with the softer terracotta ceramic floor tiles it can be a help if these tiles are sealed before they are fixed. They can always be given further coats afterwards, but it can save a lot of work if the tile has some resistance to marking before you start putting your adhesive-covered fingers all over it. This is sometimes recommended by the supplier or the manufacturer of the tiles in any case. If they recommend a particular sealant, then stick with that one. They are not likely to recommend one that will cause difficulties. If you do decide to pre-seal your tiles the easiest way is to lay them out flat and to use a new, very clean paint roller. Use one that does not hold a great deal of sealer as you don't want any surplus sealant sloshing about.

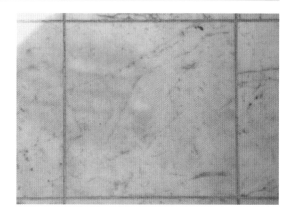

Marbles and some other natural stones can stain from behind if precautions are not taken.

You want to seal the face of the tile only. The sealant is intended to stop things staining or sticking to the face of the tiles and you don't want sealant running down the edges where it can affect the way your grout sticks to the tiles. Once the sealant has dried, fixing can start.

CHAPTER 13

Cleaning and Maintenance

Unlike many finishes, tiling, with the exception of the natural stones, tends to be reasonably idiot-proof when it comes to maintenance and most people will be well aware of the properties of the tiles when it comes to cleaning. The problems which are encountered are often the result of incorrect use of cleaning materials and the impression fostered by television commercials that 'Once over with superjiz and all your cleaning problems will disappear.' I have spent a reasonable portion of my life on my hands and knees looking at floors that were being accused of being impossible to clean or losing their colour, only to leave a quarter of an hour later with the building owner determined to sack his cleaning contractor. The simple fact is that many people expect cleaning to be easier than it actually is. A mop is an easy way of cleaning a floor, but is not all that efficient. Every so often, a floor needs to be 'bottomed out' to remove the film of combined dirt and detergent residues that build up over time.

SEALERS

A brief note here about sealers. They come in two basic types. The first type, sometimes called 'penetrating sealers', are usually based on an organic solvent and often have quite a low solids content. These are intended to soak into the pores of the material; the solvent then evaporates, leaving the solid resin behind in the pores. The idea is that the pores will then not be capable of taking in anything which might stain the material. The second type of sealer is usually water-based and has a high solids content. These do soak in to some extent, but generally the resin is deposited on the face of the material and forms a film which acts as a physical barrier to stains.

There are pros and cons for both types of sealer. The penetrating ones are designed not to affect the appearance of the tile as much as the second type, but, because some materials can vary tremendously in density, take-up can occasionally be patchy, particularly with natural stones as these vary in consistency. One part of a tile soaks up the stuff like blotting paper, while in another area it just lies on the surface. This, occasionally, can make it difficult to get the surface to look even.

The surface sealers do not have this problem to the same degree as you simply reapply them until you have an even film on the surface of the floor. In some cases this film is 'buffable', which means that it is intended to shine if you buff it up. Some can also have anti-slip properties. However, these sealers do alter the character of the finish on the tile and can look artificial. They also have to be reapplied if they wear off in busy areas. If you have used a material that calls for sealing, always stick with the type of sealer recommended by the manufacturer of the tiles and to their recommendations.

If you do decide that you want to seal your tiled floor here are a few hints and tips that they probably don't have the space on the label to tell you.

OPPOSITE: Black is a terrific colour for impact, but bear in mind that it is also the most difficult colour to keep clean.

The first tip is to make sure that the floor is clean before you seal it. The sealer bottle will say this anyway, but they really do mean *totally and immaculately* clean. If you are not completely happy with the appearance of the floor, do not seal it. The sealer will not make marks go away, but can make them nearly impossible to remove later.

Secondly, bear in mind that a sealer wears off in the areas that get the most traffic. The edges of the floor are not getting any wear, but when you when you reapply the sealer it will be over the whole floor. A year or two of this treatment and you have one coat of sealer where the floor is walked on and fifteen or twenty coats around the edges.

Liquid emulsion polishes can also have this effect, as do the 'wash and shine' cleaning products which contain a small amount of sealer/polish that is left on the floor as it dries after cleaning. This has exactly the same effect as applying a small amount of sealer every time you wash the floor, with the additional drawback that you are incorporating traces of dirt from the cleaning water. A year of mopping once a week can give you fifty-two fine layers of dirty sealer around the edges and you will be wondering why the edges and corners are looking darker and dingier than the rest of the floor. The sealer then has to be stripped and the whole floor resealed. This is neither the easiest nor most pleasant of jobs.

The point I am making is that sealers are fine if correctly used, but, like everything in life, they have their drawbacks. Many sealers, polishes and cleaners are fine products and the tiling trade uses them to advantage. But use them as and when you need them. There should be no need to apply them as a matter of routine maintenance. If you have a favourite 'clean and shine' cleaning product ask yourself if you need to use it every time you wash the floor. Remember that the manufacturers of these products make a living by selling cleaning products and sealers, not floors.

One word of warning! If you apply anything that is intended to remain on the surface of your tiling, bear in mind that you will be walking on that, not the tiling. Do not expect the slip-resistance factor of the tiles still to apply. The figures quoted for slip-resistance apply only to the clean tile face as it left the factory.

CLEANING CERAMIC TILES
Glazed Ceramic Wall Tiling

Providing it has been left clean by the tiler, glazed wall tiling needs nothing more than wiping over with a clean damp cloth with, if there is any grease present, a small amount of detergent or kitchen worktop cleaner. Dirt in joints is best removed with a small scrubbing brush. If you want to polish the tiles up remember that the glaze on a tile is basically a layer of glass and that anything which works on glass will work on a glazed tile. A damp wash leather is as good as anything.

The most common complaint about wall tiles is the joints turning black, particularly in bathrooms. This has resulted in various treatments intended either to remove the problem or to cover it up. To tackle this, you need to understand what you are dealing with. Firstly, unless you come from a family of miners who are not bothering to use the pit head baths, it is not dirt. It is the same mould that blackens wallpaper on damp walls. Bathrooms are damp places and you are giving the mould the conditions it likes. The black joints are going to happen on any tiling job that is kept damp for long enough. The mould needs little sustenance and will even grow on glass.

The best way of dealing with mould is to try not to let it start in the first place. If it does start, and it does in most bathrooms, don't give it the chance to become too established. Ventilating the bathroom and making sure that the walls dry out helps a lot; it can't grow if there is no water. Other than that, regular washing down with something which kills the mould or inhibits its growth is the only real treatment. Some of the proprietary products work quite well, but a solution of household bleach is as effective as anything. If the joints are badly affected you may have to scrub them with a fine brush. Wear rubber gloves and stick to the instructions on the bottle. You may find the effect is not instant and it takes an hour or so for the stains to fade. Occasionally you might get a brownie-pinkish coloured stain, particularly near the bottom of a shower wall or on the top lip of a shower tray. This is another micro-organism that likes the conditions. Bleach will sort this out too. The important thing is to do it on a regular basis – if you leave it twice as long as you should, it will take three times as long to get off.

Glazed Ceramic Floor Tiles

As the glaze is in fact a layer of glass there is little that needs to be done with these other than washing regularly. Using a little detergent if there is grease about and an occasional thorough scrubbing to make sure that the joints are kept clean are all that is usually required. Do not overdo the detergent – more about this later – and do not use the 'clean and shine' detergents. They give no benefit on a glazed surface and can affect the anti-slip properties. The only exception is if you feel that the joints need to be sealed for some reason.

Unglazed Floor Tiles

The vast majority of unglazed ceramic floor tiles are designed to need nothing more than hot water and a small amount of soap or detergent to keep them clean. If a tile has an anti-slip or textured finish then an occasional scrub will probably be needed to get dirt out of the indents that such tiles often have.

We have been conditioned to believe that something more than cleaning is needed for a floor to look good and that floors need to be sealed in order to look their best. If a tile has a porous open texture then sealing can have distinct advantages, but it shouldn't be assumed that it is either necessary or desirable in every case.

If you are using a porcelain or any other fully vitrified tile then sealing in any form is, technically, a waste of time. There is nothing to seal, as the tile is not going to absorb anything anyway. It may put a shine on the floor but it is the seal that is doing the shining, not the floor. A sealer can make the colour seem more intense, but this is caused by the optical effect of the shinier finish.

On open-textured or absorbent ceramics, sealing can be an advantage. In the case of terracotta it is essential. Dirt can get into fine crevices in the face of the tile and can be very difficult, sometimes impossible, to remove. Liquids can get drawn by capillary action into the body of the tile and cause staining. The whole purpose of a seal is to fill the fine crevices and pores in the tile's surface to stop this happening. Whether you go down the route of the traditional materials, such as sealing with boiled linseed oil and waxing, or one of the modern sealer and maintenance systems, bear in mind that terracotta, a bit like antique furniture, is usually so heavily protected by a layer of sealer and polish that it is this layer you will be maintaining, not the tile itself.

CLEANING NATURAL STONES

This can be a complicated subject as the range of materials is so enormous. One point to bear in mind is that synthetic detergents and sealers are relatively new. Modern detergents and sealers did not exist until quite recently and for most of history marble, slate and granite floors performed quite well simply by being washed with soap and water, as did our clothes and us.

Providing you are patient enough and are careful not to damage the floor in the meanwhile this is still quite a good way of maintaining natural stone floors. Soap contains fats which, when used in conjunction with warm water, tend to be absorbed into the surface of the floor, bring the colour up and have the effect of acting as a sealer to some degree. It also has the advantage that it is relatively easily removed with modern detergents. The downside is that it takes time to build up the finish in this manner, and we could, depending upon the area, be talking years rather than months. If you do decide to go down this route, use good-quality soap flakes and don't use too much.

However, we do live in the world of the 'instant fix' and there are many good products on the market for cleaning, sealing and polishing natural stones. These products do have some advantages in that they can give some resistance to staining and chemical attack. This is the one thing that is more likely to happen to a natural stone tile than a ceramic tile. If you are using them in a kitchen, where the chance of staining from oils is high, then sealing is a distinct advantage. It can also help to prevent a marble floor being damaged by acid.

Granite

The first thing is to decide if your tiles need a sealer in the first place. Granite, at least in polished form, is both hard and dense and except in areas that are subject to oil spillages, needs little other than regular washing. If you really do think that you need to seal a granite floor, do it very sparingly. It will probably not absorb much and if any dries on the floor surface it will look as if you have varnished it.

Slate

Slate is usually sealed, simply because it marks easily and sealing helps to prevent any unsightly stains from oil and grease. As mentioned earlier, in the 'old days' slate used to be oiled in a similar way to terracotta as a method of finishing it, in effect pre-staining it so that later marks would not show. However, this is a smelly and messy job and, depending upon what solvent you decide to use as a carrier for the oil, not one to do with a naked flame around. Whether or not you want to seal and polish a slate floor is a question that could be argued about all day. Even within the trade people have their own opinions on the subject.

With today's busy lifestyles people want a floor that is easy to maintain, or at least as easy to maintain as any particular material can be, and sealing is probably the best way of achieving this result with slate, as is does make cleaning easier. Whether or not you want to polish it is a matter of choice. Personally I am against it, but I do not expect slate to shine. I rather like the semi-matt finish that slate comes with naturally.

If you do decide to use a sealer, buy one that is recommended for slate and stick to the manufacturer's instructions. What has to be emphasized is that the floor must be *really* clean first. If you are using a plain black or green slate you will not get away with anything. Any residual cement from the fixing *must* be removed first and there are special cleaners for this purpose.

For general maintenance regular washing with a mild detergent or a little soap and clean water is all that is needed. If you do decide to use a polish, again, use one that is suitable for the material and remember that if you apply a higher finish than the material takes naturally from traffic, then you will have to maintain it.

Marble

Again, whether or not a marble floor needs a sealer is a matter of opinion. It is not the norm to seal a very highly acid-polished tile as these are usually only used in areas where there is little risk of staining and sealers can look artificial on such a highly finished surface.

A tile with a less high finish can benefit from a sealer if it is in an area where there might be a danger of staining. Although there will be people who will be making special cleaners 'just for marble', a well-laid marble floor can, in most cases, be maintained quite well simply by being washed with water with a small quantity of good-quality soap flakes added. There are plenty of marble floors about that have been cleaned this way for over a hundred years and are still looking good.

There is one word of warning that has to be given, which applies to all marble and limestone floors. *Never* use an acid cleaner, or anything else that is acid, on the floor, and if anything acid is spilled on marble or limestone, even something as seemingly innocuous as lemon juice or tonic water, wash it off straight away. Acid will burn the face of marble. Providing the damage is not too bad a tile can sometimes be refinished, but it is not something that you want to do. If oil is spilled get that off quickly too, as oil can stain if it is left on the floor.

Limestone

Every item of maintenance which applies to marble can also be applied to limestone, with the additional proviso that some limestone is so porous that sealers should generally be used unless the supplier specifically says that it is not necessary. There are some limestones that are dense enough to be treated in the same way as you would marble, but if you are in any doubt check when you buy the tiles.

Once the floor has been sealed treat it as a marble, washing with clean, warm water and a little detergent or soap.

Useful Addresses

Many books of this type contain a list of companies that supply the materials and equipment needed for the work. A list of tile shops would be long, not all that helpful, and out of date before the book is off the press. I am giving the contact details of the three main trade associations for the materials covered in this book. They have members who are suppliers to the trade and to the public. And their lists will be up to date!

The Tile Association
Forum Court
83, Copers Cope Road,
Beckenham. Kent
BR3 1NR
Tel. No: 020 8663 0946
Fax. No: 020 8663 0949
Email: info@tiles.org.uk
Website: www.tiles.org.uk

National Federation of Terrazzo Marble and Mosaic Specialists
P.O.Box 2843
London
W1A 5PG
Tel. No: 0845 609 0050
Fax: 0845 607 8610
Email: info@nftmms.co.uk
Website: www.nftmms.co.uk

Stone Federation Great Britain
Channel Business Centre
Ingles Manor, Castle Hill Avenue,
Folkestone, Kent, CT20 2RD
Tel. No. 01303 856123
Website: www.stone-federationgb.org.uk

Index